100 Recipes *from* 100 Books

Jean Paré

www.companyscoming.com
visit our website

100 Recipes from 100 Books

First Printing March 2014

Library and Archives Canada Cataloguing in Publication

Paré, Jean, author

100 recipes from 100 books / Jean Paré.

(Original series)
Includes index.
ISBN 978-1-927126-61-5 (bound)

1. Cooking. 2. Cookbooks. I. Title. II. Title: One hundred recipes from one hundred books. III. Series: Paré, Jean. Original series.

TX715.6.P356 2014 641.5 C2013-906559-8

Published by
Company's Coming Publishing Limited
2311 – 96 Street
Edmonton, Alberta, Canada T6N 1G3
Tel: 780-450-6223 Fax: 780-450-1857
www.companyscoming.com

We acknowledge the financial support of the Government of Canada through the Canada Book Fund for our publishing activities.

Printed in China

PC: 21

TABLE OF CONTENTS

THE COMPANY'S COMING STORY

Jean Paré (pronounced "jeen PAIR-ee") grew up understanding that the combination of family, friends and home cooking is the best recipe for a good life. From her mother, she learned to appreciate good cooking, while her father praised even her earliest attempts in the kitchen. When Jean left home, she took with her a love of cooking, many family recipes and an intriguing desire to read cookbooks as if they were novels!

"Never share a recipe you wouldn't use yourself."

When her four children had all reached school age, Jean volunteered to cater the 50th anniversary celebration of the Vermilion School of Agriculture, now Lakeland College, in Alberta, Canada. Working out of her home, Jean prepared a dinner for more than 1,000 people, launching a flourishing catering operation that continued for over 18 years. During that time, she had countless opportunities to test new ideas with immediate feedback—resulting in empty plates and contented customers! Whether preparing cocktail sandwiches for a house party or serving a hot meal for 1,500 people, Jean Paré earned a reputation for great food, courteous service and reasonable prices.

As requests for her recipes increased, Jean was often asked the question, "Why don't you write a cookbook?" Jean responded by teaming up with her son, Grant Lovig, in the fall of 1980 to form Company's Coming Publishing Limited. The publication of *150 Delicious Squares* on April 14, 1981 marked the debut of what would soon become one of the world's most popular cookbook series.

The company has grown since those early days when Jean worked from a spare bedroom in her home. Nowadays every Company's Coming recipe is *kitchen-tested* before it is approved for publication.

Company's Coming cookbooks are distributed in Canada, the United States, Australia and other world markets. Bestsellers many times over in English, Company's Coming cookbooks have also been published in French and Spanish.

Familiar and trusted in home kitchens around the world, Company's Coming cookbooks are offered in a variety of formats. Highly regarded as kitchen workbooks, the softcover Original Series, with its lay-flat plastic comb binding, is still a favourite among readers.

Jean Paré's approach to cooking has always called for *quick and easy recipes* using *everyday ingredients.* That view has served her well. The recipient of many awards, including the Queen Elizabeth Golden Jubilee Medal, Jean was appointed Member of the Order of Canada, her country's highest lifetime achievement honour.

Jean continues to share what she calls The Golden Rule of Cooking: *Never share a recipe you wouldn't use yourself.* It's an approach that has worked—*millions of times over!*

FOREWORD

It seemed appropriate for us, when contemplating the 100th Original Series cookbook, to make a special collectors' edition to celebrate the occasion. Jean's first book, *150 Delicious Squares,* was met with such widespread success that we were encouraged to publish more cookbooks. *Casseroles* came out in June 1982, *Muffins and More* in July 1983, *Salads* in June 1984, *Appetizers* in May 1985 and *Desserts* in April 1986. Well, we were sure off and running!

Those early books celebrated the food and food customs of Jean and her family. Over the years since then, we have continued to publish more titles in many areas to add to this very popular series of cookbooks.

Travelling had a huge effect on Jean's cooking. Many of the ideas and recipes were created as a result of her extensive globe-trotting. She always arrived home with numerous recipes and her own observations and notes, and then proceeded to her test kitchen. Jean continues to believe that good food is all about sharing, and she is happy to do it.

Jean still warmly acknowledges her fans, and signs autographs when asked, even though she says she "doesn't know what the fuss is about."

In this commemorative cookbook, we have taken a recipe out of each of the previous 99 Original Series cookbooks. To make it even more special, we have also included a recipe from our upcoming *Mexican Made Easy* Original Series cookbook, so there are truly 100 recipes from 100 cookbooks featured here.

Nutrition Information Guidelines

Each recipe is analyzed using the most current versions of the Canadian Nutrient File from Health Canada, and the United States Department of Agriculture (USDA) Nutrient Database for Standard Reference.

- If more than one ingredient is listed (such as "butter or hard margarine"), or if a range is given (1 – 2 tsp., 5 – 10 mL), only the first ingredient or first amount is analyzed.
- Milk used is 1% M.F. (milk fat), unless otherwise stated.
- Cooking oil used is canola oil, unless otherwise stated.
- Ingredients indicating "sprinkle," "optional" or "for garnish" are not included in the nutrition information.
- The fat in recipes and combination foods can vary greatly depending upon the sources and types of fats used in each specific ingredient. For these reasons, the amount of saturated, monounsaturated and polyunsaturated fats may not add up to the total fat content.

Beet Bonanza

So good, and so good for you!

Medium beets (see Tip, below)	2	2
Medium carrots	6	6
Medium English cucumber	1	1
Medium celery ribs	2	2
Small apple	1	1

Scrub vegetables. Do not peel. Cut into chunks to fit juicer feed chute. Push chunks, 1 at a time, through chute. Makes 2 1/4 cups (550 mL).

1/2 cup (125 mL): *70 Calories; 0 g Total Fat (0 g Mono, 0 g Poly, 0 g Sat); 0 mg Cholesterol; 16 g Carbohydrate; 3 g Fibre; 2 g Protein; 90 mg Sodium*

Appliance Cooking.
First published in March 2001.

TIP

Don't get caught red-handed! Wear rubber gloves when handling beets.

Coconut Fruit Smoothie

A great breakfast drink for a jump-start to the morning. Taste of the tropics.

Ripe large mango (about 12 oz., 340 g), chopped (see Tip, below)	1	1
Fresh (or whole frozen) strawberries	10	10
Medium banana (about 5 oz., 140 g), cut up	1	1
Orange juice	1 cup	1 cup
Light coconut milk	1 cup	1 cup

Put all 5 ingredients into blender. Process until smooth. Makes about 4 cups (1 L).

1 cup (250 mL): *160 Calories; 4.5 g Total Fat (0 g Mono, 0 g Poly, 3 g Sat); 0 mg Cholesterol; 31 g Carbohydrate; 3 g Fibre; 1 g Protein; 20 mg Sodium*

Rush-Hour Recipes.
First published in September 2002.

TIP

To shop for ripe mangoes, look for those that yield slightly to gentle pressure. The colouring will be deep red and/or rich yellow with only a blush of green at most. Medium to large mangoes are generally the best tasting. A ripe mango will smell fairly fruity at the stem end as long as it is not cold. Avoid product that is too small, too soft or wrinkled.

Citrus Sunburst

A refreshing, eye-catching drink bursting with orange flavour.

CITRUS CREAM		
Orange sherbet	**2 cups**	**500 mL**
Pink grapefruit juice	**2/3 cup**	**150 mL**
Can of mandarin orange segments (with juice)	**10 oz.**	**284 mL**
Ice cubes	**6**	**6**
Gin (3 oz.), optional	**6 tbsp.**	**100 mL**
Grenadine syrup	**1/2 tsp.**	**2 mL**
Lime slices, for garnish	**4**	**4**

Citrus Cream: Process first 4 ingredients in blender until smooth. Makes 3 1/2 cups (875 mL) cream.

Divide and measure gin and grenadine into 4 chilled small glasses. Pour Citrus Cream over top of each.

Garnish each with lime slice. Serves 4.

***1 serving (with alcohol):** 239 Calories; 2.1 g Total Fat (0.6 g Mono, 0.1 g Poly, 1.2 g Sat); 5 mg Cholesterol; 44 g Carbohydrate; trace Fibre; 2 g Protein; 52 mg Sodium*

The Beverage Book.
First published in October 2004.

Hazelnut Eggnog Latte

This sweet and creamy treat is a decadent way to start Christmas morning, or to welcome guests in from the cold. Balance the sweetness to your own taste by adding more or less coffee.

Hot strong prepared coffee	**5 cups**	**1.25 L**
Chocolate hazelnut spread	**1 cup**	**250 mL**
Eggnog	**4 cups**	**1 L**

Whisk coffee and chocolate hazelnut spread in large saucepan on medium until smooth.

Add eggnog. Heat and stir until hot, but not boiling. Makes about 10 cups (2.5 L).

1 cup (250 mL): *230 Calories; 12.7 g Total Fat (5.1 g Mono, 1.5 g Poly, 5.4 g Sat); 60 mg Cholesterol; 24 g Carbohydrate; 1 g Fibre; 5 g Protein; 64 mg Sodium*

Entertaining for the Holidays.
First published in October 2011.

Buttermilk Pancakes

Feathery light. Simple to make.

All-purpose flour	1 1/4 cups	300 mL
Buttermilk powder (available at grocery or health food stores)	1/3 cup	75 mL
Granulated sugar	4 tsp.	20 mL
Baking powder	2 tsp.	10 mL
Baking soda	1 tsp.	5 mL
Salt	1/4 tsp.	1 mL
Large egg, fork-beaten	1	1
Cooking oil	2 tbsp.	30 mL
Vanilla extract	1/2 tsp.	2 mL
Water	1 cup	250 mL

Measure first 6 ingredients into bowl. Stir well.

Add remaining 4 ingredients. Stir just to moisten. A few lumps are fine. Pancakes may be made thin or thick by adding more or less water. Thicker pancakes take a bit longer to cook through. Heat electric griddle or frying pan until drops of water dance around on surface. Drop batter by large tablespoonfuls onto hot greased pan. When bubbles form and edges appear dry, turn to brown other side. No need to grease pan between batches. Makes 16 pancakes, about 3 1/2 inches (9 cm) in diameter.

1 pancake: *70 Calories; 2.5 g Total Fat (1 g Mono, 0.5 g Poly, 0 g Sat); 15 mg Cholesterol; 10 g Carbohydrate; 0 g Fibre; 2 g Protein; 170 mg Sodium*

Breakfasts & Brunches.
First published in April 1998.

Buckwheat Sunrise

Watch out, oatmeal! Tangy orange and cranberry turn buckwheat into a serious contender for favourite breakfast grain. Make this dish the night before for a fast breakfast in the morning.

Water	**1 1/2 cups**	**375 mL**
Whole buckwheat	**1 cup**	**250 mL**
Grated orange zest	**1 tsp.**	**5 mL**
Salt	**1/4 tsp.**	**1 mL**
Orange juice	**1 cup**	**250 mL**
Chopped dried apricot	**1/3 cup**	**75 mL**
Dried cranberries	**1/3 cup**	**75 mL**
Liquid honey	**3 tbsp.**	**45 mL**
Slivered almonds, toasted (see Tip, page 58)	**1/4 cup**	**60 mL**

Combine first 4 ingredients in medium saucepan. Bring to a boil. Reduce heat to medium-low. Simmer, covered, for about 15 minutes, without stirring, until buckwheat is tender.

Add orange juice. Stir. Add next 3 ingredients. Stir. Transfer to medium bowl. Cool at room temperature before covering. Chill for at least 6 hours or overnight until apricot and cranberries are softened and liquid is absorbed.

Add almonds. Stir. Makes about 3 cups (750 mL).

1 cup (250 mL): *367 Calories; 6.1 g Total Fat (3.3 g Mono, 1.6 g Poly, 0.7 g Sat); 0 mg Cholesterol; 76 g Carbohydrate; 6 g Fibre; 8 g Protein; 210 mg Sodium*

Variation: Instead of dried cranberries, use same amount of chopped dried cherries.

Whole Grain Recipes.
First published in April 2011.

Mexican Egg Wraps

Taste buds still asleep? Wake them up with this combination of spicy salsa, Cheddar cheese and eggs nestled in a soft flour tortilla. This is just about the easiest and most delicious breakfast you could make.

Tub margarine	**2 tsp.**	**10 mL**
Large eggs	**4**	**4**
Salt, sprinkle		
Pepper, sprinkle		
Salsa	**1/2 cup**	**125 mL**
Whole-wheat flour tortillas (6 inch, 15 cm, diameter)	**4**	**4**
Grated light sharp Cheddar cheese	**1/4 cup**	**60 mL**
Finely chopped fresh cilantro	**1 tsp.**	**5 mL**

Melt margarine in large frying pan on medium. Break eggs, 1 at a time, into pan. Pierce yolks with fork. Sprinkle with salt and pepper. Cook, covered, for about 3 minutes until set.

Spread 2 tbsp. (30 mL) salsa on each tortilla, leaving 1 inch (2.5 cm) border. Place 1 egg over salsa on each tortilla. Sprinkle with cheese and cilantro. Fold sides over filling. Roll up from bottom to enclose filling. Makes 4 wraps.

1 wrap: *212 Calories; 9.1 g Total Fat (2.9 g Mono, 2.6 g Poly, 2.6 g Sat); 190 mg Cholesterol; 22 g Carbohydrate; 2 g Fibre; 11 g Protein; 486 mg Sodium*

30-Minute Diabetic Cooking.
First published in October 2008.

Seafood Quiche

A delightful combination of seafood, delicately seasoned with dill.

Cooked fresh (or imitation) crabmeat (about 3 oz., 85 g), chopped	**1/2 cup**	**125 mL**
Cooked small shrimp (about 3 oz., 85 g)	**1/2 cup**	**125 mL**
Smoked salmon slices (about 1 oz., 28 g), chopped	**3**	**3**
Unbaked 9 inch (23 cm) pie shell	**1**	**1**
Grated part-skim mozzarella cheese	**1 cup**	**250 mL**
Milk	**1 cup**	**250 mL**
Half-and-half cream (or homogenized milk)	**1/2 cup**	**125 mL**
Large eggs	**3**	**3**
Chopped fresh dill (or 3/4 tsp., 4 mL, dried)	**1 tbsp.**	**15 mL**
Cayenne pepper	**1/8 tsp.**	**0.5 mL**
Salt	**1/2 tsp.**	**2 mL**
Pepper	**1/8 tsp.**	**0.5 mL**
Grated Parmesan cheese (optional)	**2 tbsp.**	**30 mL**

Scatter crab, shrimp and salmon over bottom of pie shell. Sprinkle with mozzarella cheese.

Beat next 7 ingredients with whisk in medium bowl until well combined. Pour over mozzarella cheese.

Sprinkle with Parmesan cheese. Bake on bottom rack in 425°F (220°C) oven for 10 minutes. Reduce heat to 350°F (175°C). Bake for about 50 minutes until knife inserted in centre comes out almost clean. Let stand for 10 minutes before serving. Cuts into 6 wedges.

1 wedge: *274 Calories; 15.7 g Total Fat (6.1 g Mono, 1.6 g Poly, 6.7 g Sat); 166 mg Cholesterol; 14 g Carbohydrate; trace Fibre; 18 g Protein; 653 mg Sodium*

The Egg Book.
First published in May 2004.

Irish Breakfast

A complete breakfast—Irish style! You could use pastrami from the deli or leftover corned beef if you have any.

CORNED BEEF HASH		
Butter (or hard margarine)	**1 tbsp.**	**15 mL**
Finely chopped onion	**1/3 cup**	**75 mL**
Finely diced cooked peeled potato	**1 1/2 cups**	**375 mL**
Finely chopped deli corned beef (about 3 1/2 oz., 100 g)	**3/4 cup**	**175 mL**
Pepper	**1/4 tsp.**	**1 mL**
Chopped fresh chives	**2 tsp.**	**10 mL**
POACHED EGGS		
Water, approximately	**4 cups**	**1 L**
White vinegar	**2 tsp.**	**10 mL**
Large eggs	**4**	**4**
Chopped fresh chives	**1 tsp.**	**5 mL**
Pepper, sprinkle		

Corned Beef Hash: Melt butter in medium frying pan on medium. Add onion. Cook for about 3 minutes, stirring occasionally, until onion is starting to brown.

Add potato. Cook for about 5 minutes, stirring occasionally, until potato is golden.

Add corned beef and pepper. Heat and stir for about 1 minute until corned beef is heated through. Add chives. Stir. Makes about 1 1/2 cups (375 mL) Corned Beef Hash. Remove from heat. Cover to keep warm.

(continued on next page)

Table For Two.
First published in February 2009.

Poached Eggs: Pour water into medium saucepan until 1 1/2 inches (3.8 cm) deep. Add vinegar. Stir. Bring to a boil. Reduce heat to medium. Water should continue to simmer. Break 1 egg into shallow dish. Slip egg into water. Repeat with remaining eggs. Cook for 2 to 3 minutes until egg whites are set and yolks reach desired doneness. Transfer eggs with slotted spoon to paper towels to drain. Spoon corned beef mixture onto 2 plates. Top with eggs.

Sprinkle with chives and pepper. Serves 2.

__1 serving:__ 356 Calories; 16.2 g Total Fat (1.5 g Mono, 0.3 g Poly, 7.5 g Sat); 471 mg Cholesterol; 28 g Carbohydrate; 3 g Fibre; 23 g Protein; 803 mg Sodium

Huevos Rancheros Casserole

A hearty and satisfying Mexican-style casserole that the whole family love! Loaded with eggs, corn and beans, and topped with a refreshin colour from avocado and tomato.

Can of black beans, rinsed and drained	**19 oz.**	**540 mL**
Fresh (or frozen, thawed) kernel corn	**1 cup**	**250 mL**
Salsa	**1 cup**	**250 mL**
Large eggs	**10**	**10**
Finely chopped green onion	**2 tbsp.**	**30 mL**
Milk	**2 tbsp.**	**30 mL**
Salt	**1/8 tsp.**	**0.5 mL**
Grated medium Cheddar cheese	**1 cup**	**250 mL**
Chopped avocado	**1/2 cup**	**125 mL**
Chopped tomato	**1/2 cup**	**125 mL**
Crushed tortilla chips	**1/4 cup**	**60 mL**
Chopped fresh cilantro (or parsley)	**2 tsp.**	**10 mL**

Combine first 3 ingredients in greased shallow 2 quart (2 L) casserole.

Whisk next 4 ingredients in medium bowl. Pour over black bean mixture.

Sprinkle with cheese. Bake, uncovered, in 350°F (175°C) oven for about 50 minutes until set and golden.

Scatter remaining 4 ingredients, in order given, over top. Serve immediately. Serves 8.

1 serving: *250 Calories; 12.0 g Total Fat (3.5 g Mono, 1.0 g Poly, 4.5 g Sat); 185 mg Cholesterol; 23 g Carbohydrate; 6 g Fibre; 15 g Protein; 530 mg Sodium*

Anytime Casseroles.
First published in February 2011.

Breakfast Split

Dessert for breakfast—does it get any better than that? Have your backpack ready so you can "split" as soon as you're done with breakfast.

Get It Together: dry measures, ice cream scoop, dessert bowl, cutting board, sharp knife

1. Vanilla frozen yogurt	**3/4 cup**	**175 mL**
2. Medium banana	**1**	**1**
3. Chopped fresh strawberries	**1/4 cup**	**60 mL**
Fresh raspberries	**1/4 cup**	**60 mL**
Granola	**1/4 cup**	**60 mL**

1. Put the frozen yogurt into the bowl.

2. Cut the banana in half crosswise. Cut both halves lengthwise into 2 pieces, for a total of 4 pieces. Arrange around the frozen yogurt in the bowl.

3. Sprinkle with the berries and granola. Serves 1.

1 serving: *472 Calories; 13.4 g Total Fat (3.6 g Mono, 5 g Poly, 4.2 g Sat); 11 mg Cholesterol; 82 g Carbohydrate; 7 g Fibre; 14 g Protein; 117 mg Sodium*

Bright Idea: What's your favourite fresh or canned fruit? Use that instead of the berries.

Kids' Healthy Cooking.
First published in July 2006.

Baked Breakfast Pears

This elegant dish is deceptively easy to prepare and is a welcome break from standard breakfast fare. Pears are available year-round but are in season from June to February, and there are many varieties to choose from. Bosc pears are one of the most popular for baking and poaching because they keep their shape when cooked.

Large, ripe, firm pears	**4**	**4**
Lemon juice	**1 tbsp.**	**15 mL**
Cinnamon sticks, broken in half	**2**	**2**
Agave syrup	**2 tbsp.**	**30 mL**
Apple juice	**1/3 cup**	**75 mL**
Vanilla bean	**1/2**	**1/2**
Vanilla Greek yogurt	**1 cup**	**250 mL**
Chopped apple	**2 tbsp.**	**30 mL**
Chopped walnuts, toasted (see Tip, page 58)	**2 tbsp.**	**30 mL**
Cooking spray		

Preheat oven to 350°F (175°C). Spray 9 x 13 inch (23 x 33 cm) baking dish with cooking spray. Halve pears and core, removing a 1 inch (2.5 cm) deep scoop. Brush halves with lemon juice.

Combine next 3 ingredients in small bowl. Cut vanilla bean in half and scrape seeds into baking dish. Arrange pears, cut side up, in single layer in dish. Bake for 40 to 45 minutes, basting pears with apple juice mixture a few times, until pears are tender. Remove from oven and allow to cool completely. Cover and chill for at least 6 hours or overnight, turning pears in liquid at least twice during chilling time.

To serve, combine yogurt and apple. Spoon mixture into pear halves and sprinkle with walnuts. Serves 8.

1 serving: *130 Calories; 4 g Total Fat (0 g Mono, 1 g Poly, 2 g Sat); 5 mg Cholesterol; 24 g Carbohydrate; 3 g Fibre; 2 g Protein; 20 mg Sodium*

Breakfasts On the Go.
First published in July 2013.

Boston Brown Bread

Historically eaten with Boston baked beans, this bread is wonderful with stew or even with coffee.

Cornmeal	**2 cups**	**500 mL**
All-purpose flour	**1 1/2 cups**	**375 mL**
Salt	**1 tsp.**	**5 mL**
Buttermilk, fresh or reconstituted from powder	**1 cup**	**250 mL**
Fancy (mild) molasses	**1 cup**	**250 mL**
Baking soda	**1 tsp.**	**5 mL**
Hot water	**2 tsp.**	**10 mL**
Buttermilk, fresh or reconstituted from powder	**1 cup**	**250 mL**

Measure cornmeal, flour and salt into large bowl. Stir.

Add first amount of buttermilk and molasses. Stir well.

Stir baking soda into hot water in small cup. Add to batter. Mix well.

Mix in second amount of buttermilk. Turn into 2 greased 28 oz. (796 mL) cans, or 3 greased 19 oz. (540 mL) cans, or 1 greased 2 quart (2 L) casserole dish. Fill 2/3 full. Cover with foil. Secure foil with string. Place cans or dish in steamer with boiling water halfway up sides of containers. Cover steamer. Return water to a boil. Steam for 2 hours. Add more boiling water as needed to keep level up. Remove cans from water. Let stand 5 minutes before removing bread from cans. Serve sliced, either warm or cold. Makes 2 or 3 cans or one 2 quart (2 L) casserole. Cuts into 32 slices.

1 slice: *90 Calories; 0 g Total Fat (0 g Mono, 0 g Poly, 0 g Sat); 0 mg Cholesterol; 21 g Carbohydrate; 0 g Fibre; 1 g Protein; 140 mg Sodium*

Breads.
First published in August 1996.

Bran Muffins

Can easily be doubled for freezing. Top notch. Gail's favourite.

All-purpose flour	**1 cup**	**250 mL**
Baking powder	**1 tsp.**	**5 mL**
Baking soda	**1 tsp.**	**5 mL**
Salt	**1/2 tsp.**	**2 mL**
Raisins	**3/4 cup**	**175 mL**
Buttermilk (or soured milk, see Tip, below)	**1 cup**	**250 mL**
Natural bran	**1 cup**	**250 mL**
Cooking oil	**1/3 cup**	**75 mL**
Fancy (mild) molasses	**3 tbsp.**	**45 mL**
Large egg	**1**	**1**
Brown sugar, packed	**1/4 cup**	**60 mL**
Vanilla extract	**1/2 tsp.**	**2 mL**

In large bowl combine flour, baking powder, soda, salt and raisins. Stir well. Push up around sides of bowl making well in centre.

In another bowl stir buttermilk with bran. Let stand 5 minutes.

Add remaining ingredients to bran mixture in order given. Beat with spoon until mixed. Pour into well. Stir just to moisten. Batter will be lumpy. Fill greased muffin cups 3/4 full. Bake in 375°F (190°C) oven for 20 to 25 minutes. Let stand 5 minutes. Remove from pan. Makes 12.

1 muffin: *180 Calories; 7 g Total Fat (4 g Mono, 1.5 g Poly, 0.5 g Sat); 20 mg Cholesterol; 29 g Carbohydrate; 3 g Fibre; 3 g Protein; 260 mg Sodium*

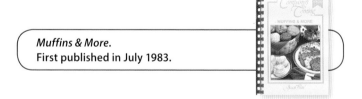

Muffins & More.
First published in July 1983.

TIP

To make soured milk, measure 1 tbsp. (15 mL) white vinegar or lemon juice into a 1 cup (250 mL) liquid measure. Add enough milk to make 1 cup (250 mL). Stir. Let stand for 1 minute.

Cranberry Sparkle Muffins

Use different colours of sparkling sanding sugar to correspond with a holiday or special occasion. Tart cranberries are a wonderful contrast to the sweetness.

All-purpose flour	2 cups	500 mL
Baking powder	1 tbsp.	15 mL
Salt	1/2 tsp.	2 mL
Butter (or hard margarine), softened	1/4 cup	60 mL
Granulated sugar	1/2 cup	125 mL
Large eggs	2	2
Vanilla (or plain) yogurt	1 cup	250 mL
Chopped fresh (or frozen) cranberries	1 cup	250 mL
TOPPING		
White sanding (decorating) sugar (see Note)	2 tbsp.	30 mL
Ground cinnamon	1/4 tsp.	1 mL

Measure first 3 ingredients into large bowl. Stir. Make a well in centre.

Cream butter and granulated sugar in medium bowl. Add eggs 1 at a time, beating well after each addition. Add yogurt. Stir. Add to well.

Add cranberries. Stir until just moistened. Fill 12 greased muffin cups 3/4 full.

Topping: Combine sanding sugar and cinnamon in small cup. Sprinkle on batter. Bake in 375°F (190°C) oven for 18 to 20 minutes until wooden pick inserted in centre of muffin comes out clean. Let stand in pan for 5 minutes before removing to wire rack to cool. Makes 12 muffins.

1 muffin: *196 Calories; 5.6 g Total Fat (1.6 g Mono, 0.4 g Poly, 3.1 g Sat); 48 mg Cholesterol; 33 g Carbohydrate; 1 g Fibre; 4 g Protein; 257 mg Sodium*

Note: Sanding sugar is a coarse decorating sugar that comes in white and various colours and is available at specialty kitchen stores.

Mostly Muffins.
First published in September 2006.

Lemon Pepper Muffins

The peppery bursts of flavour in these fresh-tasting lemon muffins make them a perfect companion for fish or seafood soups and salads. If you don't have seasoned salt, table salt can be used in a pinch.

All-purpose flour	**2 1/4 cups**	**550 mL**
Baking powder	**2 1/2 tsp.**	**12 mL**
Pepper	**1 1/2 tsp.**	**7 mL**
Seasoned salt	**1/4 tsp.**	**1 mL**
Large eggs, fork-beaten	**3**	**3**
Milk	**2/3 cup**	**150 mL**
Butter (or hard margarine), melted	**1/2 cup**	**125 mL**
Granulated sugar	**1/4 cup**	**60 mL**
Lemon juice	**3 tbsp.**	**45 mL**
Grated lemon zest (see Tip, page 156)	**2 tsp.**	**10 mL**
Chopped green onion	**1/4 cup**	**60 mL**

Preheat oven to 400°F (205°C). Measure first 4 ingredients into medium bowl. Stir. Make a well in centre.

Combine next 6 ingredients in small bowl. Add to well.

Add green onion. Stir until just moistened. Fill 24 greased mini-muffin cups 3/4 full. Bake for about 12 minutes until wooden pick inserted in centre of muffin comes out clean. Let stand in pan for 5 minutes. Remove muffins from pan and place on wire rack to cool. Makes 24 mini-muffins.

1 mini-muffin: *93 Calories; 4.5 g Total Fat (1.3 g Mono, 0.2 g Poly, 2.6 g Sat); 34 mg Cholesterol; 11 g Carbohydrate; trace Fibre; 2 g Protein; 80 mg Sodium*

30-Minute Rookie Cook.
First published in September 2007.

Zucchini Cheddar Bacon Bread

A dense, moist bread with delicious bacon bites—another way to use up garden zucchini! Serve with soup for lunch or a light dinner.

All-purpose flour	1 cup	250 mL
Whole-wheat flour	1 cup	250 mL
Grated sharp Cheddar cheese	1/4 cup	60 mL
Baking powder	2 tsp.	10 mL
Baking soda	1/2 tsp.	2 mL
Salt	1/4 tsp.	1 mL
Pepper	1/4 tsp.	1 mL
Large eggs, fork-beaten	2	2
Grated zucchini (with peel)	1 1/2 cups	375 mL
Buttermilk (or soured milk, see Tip, page 32)	3/4 cup	175 mL
Bacon slices, cooked crisp and crumbled	2	2
Canola oil	2 tbsp.	30 mL
Thinly sliced green onion	2 tbsp.	30 mL
Boiling water	2 cups	500 mL

Combine first 7 ingredients in large bowl. Make a well in centre.

Combine next 6 ingredients in medium bowl. Add to well. Stir until just moistened. Spread evenly in greased 8 inch (20 cm) springform pan. Put an even layer (2 to 3 inches, 5 to 7.5 cm, thick) of crumpled foil into bottom of 5 to 7 quart (5 to 7 L) slow cooker. Pour boiling water into slow cooker. Place pan on foil, pushing down gently to settle evenly. Place double layer of tea towel over slow cooker liner. Cover with lid. Cook on High for about 2 1/2 hours until wooden pick inserted in centre comes out clean. Transfer pan to wire rack. Cool. Cuts into 12 wedges.

1 wedge: *129 Calories; 4.9 g Total Fat (2.2 g Mono, 1.0 g Poly, 1.3 g Sat); 40 mg Cholesterol; 17 g Carbohydrate; 2 g Fibre; 5 g Protein; 259 mg Sodium*

Healthy Slow Cooker.
First published in November 2010.

Parmesan Pesto Grissini

Grissini *is the Italian term for breadsticks. This recipe uses only a few ingredients to create a broadly appealing snack, appetizer or companion for a warm bowl of soup.*

Package of puff pastry, thawed according to package directions	14 oz.	397 g
Basil pesto	1/4 cup	60 mL
Balsamic vinegar	1 tbsp.	15 mL
Grated Parmesan cheese	1/2 cup	125 mL
Large egg, fork-beaten	1	1

Roll out half of pastry on lightly floured surface to 8 x 14 inch (20 x 35 cm) rectangle. Chill remaining pastry.

Combine pesto and vinegar in small bowl. Spread over pastry. Sprinkle with cheese. Roll out remaining pastry on lightly floured surface to 8 x 14 inch (20 x 35 cm) rectangle. Place over cheese. Roll gently with rolling pin to press together. Cut crosswise into twenty-four 1/2 x 8 inch (1.2 x 20 cm) strips. Loosely twist strips. Arrange about 2 inches (5 cm) apart on parchment paper-lined baking sheets.

Brush with egg. Bake in 400°F (205°C) oven for about 20 minutes until puffed and golden. Makes 24 grissini.

***1 grissini:** 120 Calories; 8.0 g Total Fat (4.0 g Mono, 1.0 g Poly, 2.0 g Sat); 10 mg Cholesterol; 8 g Carbohydrate; 0 g Fibre; 2 g Protein; 95 mg Sodium*

Everyday Italian.
First published in December 2011.

Blue Cheeseburgers

Mini-burgers are all the rage these days—this version serves up bold blue cheese flavour, nicely complemented by a sweet chutney mayonnaise.

Large egg, fork-beaten	**1**	**1**
Crumbled blue cheese	**1/4 cup**	**60 mL**
Fine dry bread crumbs	**1/4 cup**	**60 mL**
Finely chopped walnuts, toasted (see Tip, page 58)	**1/4 cup**	**60 mL**
Worcestershire sauce	**1 tbsp.**	**15 mL**
Pepper	**1/2 tsp.**	**2 mL**
Garlic powder	**1/4 tsp.**	**1 mL**
Lean ground beef	**1 lb.**	**454 g**
Mayonnaise	**1/4 cup**	**60 mL**
Mango chutney, chopped	**1 tbsp.**	**15 mL**
Mini-buns, split	**8**	**8**

Combine first 7 ingredients in large bowl.

Add beef. Mix well. Divide into 8 equal portions. Shape into 2 inch (5 cm) diameter patties. Arrange on greased baking sheet with sides. Broil on top rack in oven for about 3 minutes per side until no longer pink inside.

Combine mayonnaise and chutney in small bowl. Spread over bottom halves of buns. Place patties on mayonnaise mixture. Cover with top halves of buns. Makes 8 burgers.

1 burger: *402 Calories; 26.7 g Total Fat (0.9 g Mono, 1.9 g Poly, 7.3 g Sat); 71 mg Cholesterol; 24 g Carbohydrate; 1 g Fibre; 15 g Protein; 311 mg Sodium*

Appetizers & Snacks.
First published in October 2012.

Mushroom Turnovers

One of the tastiest appetizers ever. May be frozen baked or unbaked. Absolutely delectable.

CREAM CHEESE PASTRY		
Block cream cheese	8 oz.	250 g
Butter (or hard margarine)	1/2 cup	125 mL
All-purpose flour	1 1/2 cups	375 mL
FILLING		
Butter (or hard margarine)	3 tbsp.	45 mL
Large onion, finely chopped	1	1
Fresh mushrooms, chopped (see Note)	1/2 lb.	225 g
All-purpose flour	2 tbsp.	30 mL
Salt	1 tsp.	5 mL
Pepper	1/4 tsp.	1 mL
Ground thyme	1/4 tsp.	1 mL
Sour cream	1/4 cup	60 mL
Large egg, beaten	1	1

Cream Cheese Pastry: Have cheese and butter at room temperature. Put into bowl and beat together well. Mix in flour. Shape into ball. Chill at least 1 hour.

Filling: Combine butter, onion and mushrooms in frying pan. Sauté about 10 minutes until tender.

Add flour, salt, pepper and thyme. Stir together. Add sour cream. Stir until thickened. Remove from heat. Cool thoroughly.

Roll pastry fairly thin. Cut into 3-inch (7.5 cm) rounds. Place 1 tsp. (5 mL) filling in centre of each circle. Dampen outer half edge with beaten egg. Fold over and press edges together with fork or fingers to seal. Arrange on greased baking sheet. Cut tiny slits in top of each.

(continued on next page)

Appetizers.
First published in May 1985.

Brush tops with beaten egg. Bake in 450°F (230°C) oven for about 10 minutes or until golden brown. Makes 3 to 4 dozen.

1 turnover: *60 Calories; 5 g Total Fat (1 g Mono, 0 g Poly, 3.5 g Sat); 20 mg Cholesterol; 2 g Carbohydrate; 0 g Fibre; less than 1 g Protein; 95 mg Sodium*

Note: To use canned sliced mushrooms rather than fresh, drain and chop two 10 oz. (284 mL) cans and add to onion. Just as delicious and always on hand.

To Freeze Ahead: Do not brush with egg. Freeze on tray. Transfer frozen turnovers to carton or plastic bag. Before serving, arrange on greased baking sheet. Brush with egg. Prick holes in tops. Bake in 350°F (175°C) oven for about 20 to 30 minutes until browned. If already cooked, heat in 325°F (160°C) oven for 15 to 20 minutes until hot.

Kidney Bean Dip

If you're into "hot," you can add more cayenne pepper to this dip. It has a good flavour and an attractive browned top. Serve with tortilla chips, raw vegetables or corn chips.

BOTTOM LAYER		
Cans of kidney beans, drained	**2 x 14 oz.**	**2 x 398 mL**
Salsa	**6 tbsp.**	**100 mL**
Sliced green onion	**1/2 cup**	**125 mL**
Chili powder	**1 tsp.**	**5 mL**
Onion powder	**1/2 tsp.**	**2 mL**
Garlic powder	**1/4 tsp.**	**1 mL**
White vinegar	**1 tsp.**	**5 mL**
Parsley flakes	**2 tsp.**	**10 mL**
Cayenne pepper	**1/4 tsp.**	**1 mL**
Salt	**1/2 tsp.**	**2 mL**
TOP LAYER		
Grated medium Cheddar cheese	**1 cup**	**250 mL**
Grated Monterey Jack cheese	**1 cup**	**250 mL**
Chili powder	**1 tsp.**	**5 mL**

Bottom Layer: Mash kidney beans with fork in medium bowl.

Add next 9 ingredients. Mix well. Spread in ungreased 9 inch (23 cm) pie plate or shallow casserole.

Top Layer: Sprinkle with layer of Cheddar cheese, followed by layer of Monterey Jack cheese. Sprinkle with chili powder. Bake, uncovered, in 350°F (175°C) oven for about 30 minutes. Makes about 4 cups (1 L).

***1 tbsp. (15 mL):** 25 Calories; 1 g Total Fat (0 g Mono, 0 g Poly, 0.5 g Sat); less than 5 mg Cholesterol; 2 g Carbohydrate; 1 g Fibre; 2 g Protein; 70 mg Sodium*

Starters.
First published in November 1999.

Red Pepper Bruschetta

Small pieces of toasted bread rounds topped with sweet roasted peppers and feta cheese.

Medium red pepper, quartered	**1**	**1**
Medium yellow pepper, quartered	**1**	**1**
Finely chopped fresh parsley (or 1 1/2 tsp., 7 mL, flakes)	**2 tbsp.**	**30 mL**
Finely chopped red onion	**2 tbsp.**	**30 mL**
Olive (or cooking) oil	**1 tbsp.**	**15 mL**
Red wine vinegar	**2 tsp.**	**10 mL**
Granulated sugar	**1/2 tsp.**	**2 mL**
Salt	**1/4 tsp.**	**1 mL**
Pepper, just a pinch		
Baguette bread loaf, cut diagonally into 1/2 inch (12 mm) slices (about 30)	**1**	**1**
Olive (or cooking) oil	**2 tbsp.**	**30 mL**
Garlic clove, halved	**1**	**1**
Feta cheese, crumbled (about 1 cup, 250 mL)	**4 1/2 oz.**	**125 g**

Preheat gas barbecue to high. Cook peppers on greased grill for 10 to 15 minutes until skins are blackened and blistered. Place in bowl or resealable freezer bag. Cover or seal. Let stand for 10 minutes. Peel and discard skins. Chop peppers finely. Put into medium bowl.

Add next 7 ingredients. Stir. Cover. Chill for 1 hour. Makes 1 cup (250 mL) pepper mixture.

Brush both sides of each baguette slice with second amount of olive oil. Toast on both sides on grill over low heat.

Rub 1 side of each slice with garlic. Divide pepper mixture over garlic sides.

Sprinkle with feta cheese. Makes about 30 bruschetta.

***1 bruschetta:** 48 Calories; 2.5 g Total Fat (1.3 g Mono, 0.2 g Poly, 0.9 g Sat); 4 mg Cholesterol; 5 g Carbohydrate; trace Fibre; 1 g Protein; 114 mg Sodium*

Year-Round Grilling.
First published in March 2003.

Blue Chicken Wings

Way better for you than the deep-fried restaurant variety! Chicken drumettes are the meatiest part of the chicken wing, so you get a better meat-to-fat ratio. This recipe also gives you a delicious homemade chicken stock. Simply chill the cooking liquid overnight, then remove and discard any fat before using.

Water	6 cups	1.5 L
Chicken drumettes	3 lbs.	1.4 kg
Medium carrots, quartered	2	2
Medium onion, quartered	1	1
Bay leaf	1	1
Apricot jam	1/4 cup	60 mL
Louisiana hot sauce	2 tbsp.	30 mL
Salt	1/4 tsp.	1 mL
LIGHT BLUE DIP		
95% fat-free spreadable cream cheese	1/4 cup	60 mL
Crumbled blue cheese	1/4 cup	60 mL
Light sour cream	1/4 cup	60 mL
Chopped chives (or green onion)	3 tbsp.	45 mL

Combine first 5 ingredients in Dutch oven or large pot. Bring to a boil. Reduce heat to medium. Simmer, uncovered, for about 20 minutes until drumettes are no longer pink inside. Strain cooking liquid into medium bowl. Reserve for another use. Remove and discard carrot, onion and bay leaf.

Stir next 3 ingredients in large bowl. Add hot drumettes. Toss until jam is melted and drumettes are coated. Transfer to greased foil-lined baking sheet with sides, reserving apricot mixture in bowl. Bake in 450°F (230°C) oven for about 20 minutes, turning occasionally, until browned. Toss drumettes in remaining apricot mixture. Makes about 28 chicken wings.

Light Blue Dip: Combine all 4 ingredients in small bowl. Makes about 2/3 cup (150 mL) dip. Serve with wings.

BEFORE: 1 drumette and 1 tsp. (5 mL) dip: *230 Calories; 18 g Total Fat (5 g Sat); 430 mg Sodium*

AFTER: 1 drumette and 1 tsp. (5 mL) dip: *120 Calories; 8 g Total Fat (3 g Mono, 1.5 g Poly, 2.5 g Sat); 39 mg Cholesterol; 2 g Carbohydrate; 0 g Fibre; 10 g Protein; 114 mg Sodium*

Healthy Recipe Makeovers.
First published in December 2011.

Mushroom Salad Rolls

A filling of mushrooms, bamboo shoots and Thai condiments wrapped in rice paper. Rice paper rounds are available in the Asian section of grocery stores or in specialty Asian stores. If you cannot find shiitake or oyster mushrooms, substitute equal amounts of brown mushrooms.

Cooking oil	**1 tsp.**	**5 mL**
Thinly sliced fresh shiitake mushrooms	**1 cup**	**250 mL**
Thinly sliced fresh oyster mushrooms	**1 cup**	**250 mL**
Canned shoestring-style bamboo shoots, drained	**1/2 cup**	**125 mL**
Finely chopped onion	**1/4 cup**	**60 mL**
Sliced green onion	**1/4 cup**	**60 mL**
Finely grated ginger root (or 1/2 tsp., 2 mL, ground ginger)	**2 tsp.**	**10 mL**
Garlic clove, minced (or 1/4 tsp., 1 mL, powder)	**1**	**1**
Hoisin sauce	**2 tbsp.**	**30 mL**
Lime juice	**1 tbsp.**	**15 mL**
Soy sauce	**1 tbsp.**	**15 mL**
Chili paste (sambal oelek)	**1/2 tsp.**	**2 mL**
Rice paper rounds (6 inch, 15 cm, diameter)	**6**	**6**
Small butter lettuce leaves	**6**	**6**

Heat cooking oil in large frying pan on medium. Add next 7 ingredients. Cook for about 5 minutes, stirring occasionally, until mushrooms release their liquid.

Add next 4 ingredients. Heat and stir for 1 minute. Remove from heat. Let stand for 10 minutes.

Place 1 rice paper round in pie plate or shallow bowl of hot water until just softened. Place on work surface. Place 1 lettuce leaf on round. Spoon about 1/4 cup (60 mL) mushroom mixture over lettuce. Fold sides over filling. Roll up tightly from bottom to enclose filling. Place on plate. Cover with damp paper towel. Repeat with remaining rounds, lettuce and mushroom mixture. Makes 6 rolls.

1 roll: *35 Calories; 1 g Total Fat (0.5 g Mono, 0 g Poly, 0 g Sat); 0 mg Cholesterol; 5 g Carbohydrate; trace Fibre; 2 g Protein; 250 mg Sodium*

Vegetarian.
First published in February 2013.

Chili Cheese Bean Dip

A sourdough bread bowl holds a peppery cheese dip. You can vary the heat by your choice of salsa. Add vegetable sticks or crackers to the plate, along with the bread cubes, for dipping.

Can of romano beans, rinsed and drained	**19 oz.**	**540 mL**
Salsa	**1 cup**	**250 mL**
Diced process cheese loaf (such as Velveeta)	**3/4 cup**	**175 mL**
Block cream cheese, softened and cut up	**4 oz.**	**125 g**
Diced green pepper	**1/4 cup**	**60 mL**
Sliced green onion	**1/4 cup**	**60 mL**
Chili powder	**2 tsp.**	**10 mL**
Garlic clove, minced (or 1/4 tsp., 1 mL, powder), optional	**1**	**1**
Dried crushed chilies	**1/4 tsp.**	**1 mL**
Sourdough bread loaf (about 8 inch, 20 cm, diameter)	**1**	**1**
Chopped fresh cilantro or parsley (optional)	**2 tsp.**	**10 mL**

Coarsely mash beans with fork in large bowl.

Add next 8 ingredients. Stir well.

Cut 1/2 to 3/4 inch (1.2 to 2 cm) from top of bread loaf. Set aside top. Remove bread from inside of loaf, leaving about 3/4 inch (2 cm) thick shell. Set aside removed bread. Spoon cheese mixture into hollowed loaf. Replace top. Wrap loaf with foil. Bake in 300°F (150°C) oven for about 2 hours until heated through and cheese is melted. Remove from oven. Discard foil. Remove loaf to large serving plate. Remove top of loaf. Break up and use for dipping.

Sprinkle cilantro over cheese mixture. Cut reserved bread into bite-size pieces for dipping. Arrange around loaf. Serves 10.

***1 serving:** 268 Calories; 10.3 g Total Fat (3.1 g Mono, 0.7 g Poly, 5.7 g Sat); 25 mg Cholesterol; 34 g Carbohydrate; 4 g Fibre; 11 g Protein; 778 mg Sodium*

Potluck Dishes.
First published in September 2005.

Red-Peppered Chorizo

This creamy sausage and cheese mixture tastes great on crisp crackers or crostini slices for a hearty snack or appetizer. Goat cheese and zesty orange pair well with the spicy sausage.

Chorizo (or hot Italian) sausage, casing removed	**1 1/2 lbs.**	**680 g**
Jar of roasted red peppers, drained, chopped	**12 oz.**	**340 mL**
Balsamic vinaigrette dressing	**2 tbsp.**	**30 mL**
Frozen concentrated orange juice, thawed	**2 tbsp.**	**30 mL**
Goat (chèvre) cheese	**1/3 cup**	**75 mL**

Scramble-fry sausage in large frying pan on medium-high for about 12 minutes until no longer pink. Drain. Transfer to 3 1/2 to 4 quart (3.5 to 4 L) slow cooker.

Add next 3 ingredients. Stir. Cook, covered, on Low for 3 to 4 hours or on High for 1 1/2 to 2 hours.

Add cheese. Stir until melted. Makes about 2 1/2 cups (625 mL).

1/4 cup (60 mL): *304 Calories; 20.2 g Total Fat (8.5 g Mono, 2.3 g Poly, 7.6 g Sat); 42 mg Cholesterol; 11 g Carbohydrate; trace Fibre; 16 g Protein; 1191 mg Sodium*

5-Ingredient Slow Cooker Recipes.
First published in August 2009.

Spiced Toffee Nuts

A deliciously spiced mix of nuts in a crunchy toffee coating. A tempting nut brittle that won't stay around for long.

Egg white (large)	**1**	**1**
Whole almonds, toasted (see Tip, below)	**1 cup**	**250 mL**
Pecan halves, toasted (see Tip, below)	**1 cup**	**250 mL**
Hazelnuts (filberts), toasted (see Tip, below)	**1 cup**	**250 mL**
Granulated sugar	**2/3 cup**	**150 mL**
Liquid honey	**1/2 cup**	**125 mL**
Ground cinnamon	**1 tsp.**	**5 mL**
Ground ginger	**1 tsp.**	**5 mL**
Ground nutmeg	**1 tsp.**	**5 mL**
Salt	**3/4 tsp.**	**4 mL**

Beat egg white in medium bowl until frothy.

Add remaining 9 ingredients. Mix well. Spread on greased baking sheet. Bake in 350°F (175°C) oven for about 20 minutes, stirring 2 to 3 times, until browned. Spread out so nuts are in single layer. Cool completely. Break into bite-size pieces. Makes 3 1/3 cups (825 mL).

1/3 cup (75 mL): *310 Calories; 21 g Total Fat (13 g Mono, 4.5 g Poly, 1.5 g Sat); 0 mg Cholesterol; 31 g Carbohydrate; 4 g Fibre; 6 g Protein; 160 mg Sodium*

Sweet Cravings.
First published in November 2002.

TIP

When toasting nuts, seeds or coconut, cooking times will vary for each type of nut—so never toast them together. For small amounts, place ingredient in an ungreased shallow frying pan. Heat on medium for 3 to 5 minutes, stirring often, until golden. For larger amounts, spread ingredient evenly in an ungreased shallow pan. Bake in a 350°F (175°C) oven for 5 to 10 minutes, stirring or shaking often, until golden.

Summer Crunch Salad

A bright, beautiful salad with a fresh mix of ingredients and just the right amount of dressing. The spiced croutons add a nice crunch to the soft greens.

CROUTONS		
Butter (or hard margarine), melted	**3 tbsp.**	**45 mL**
Garlic salt	**1/4–1/2 tsp.**	**1–2 mL**
Chili powder	**1/4–1/2 tsp.**	**1–2 mL**
Celery salt	**1/4 tsp.**	**1 mL**
Unsliced white bread loaf, crust removed, cut into 1/2 inch (12 mm) cubes	**1/4**	**1/4**
Mixed salad greens	**6 cups**	**1.5 L**
Jar of roasted red peppers, drained and coarsely chopped	**13 oz.**	**370 mL**
Large avocado, coarsely chopped	**1**	**1**
Thinly sliced red onion	**1/2 cup**	**125 mL**
Small pitted ripe whole olives	**1/3 cup**	**75 mL**
RED CURRANT DRESSING		
Olive (or cooking) oil	**1/4–1/3 cup**	**60–75 mL**
White wine vinegar	**3 tbsp.**	**45 mL**
Redcurrant jelly	**2–3 tbsp.**	**30–45 mL**
Grainy mustard	**1 tbsp.**	**15 mL**
Salt	**1/4 tsp.**	**1 mL**
Pepper, just a pinch		

Croutons: Combine first 4 ingredients in large bowl. Add bread. Toss until coated. Arrange in single layer on lightly greased baking sheet. Bake in 375°F (190°C) oven for about 15 minutes, stirring once, until golden and crisp. Cool.

Put next 5 ingredients into separate large bowl. Toss gently.

Red Currant Dressing: Process all 6 ingredients in blender until smooth. Makes 3/4 cup (175 mL) dressing. Drizzle over salad green mixture. Add croutons. Toss gently. Makes about 9 cups (2.25 L).

1 cup (250 mL): *204 Calories; 15.8 g Total Fat (10.4 g Mono, 1.7 g Poly, 2.5 g Sat); trace Cholesterol; 15 g Carbohydrate; 2 g Fibre; 3 g Protein; 376 mg Sodium*

Garden Greens.
First published in May 2003.

Cobb Salad

A contribution to the salad world from California. Try your flair for arranging vegetables. This recipe is not as complicated as it looks.

DRESSING		
White vinegar	1/3 cup	75 mL
Salt	1 tsp.	5 mL
Pepper	1/4 tsp.	1 mL
Dry mustard	1/2 tsp.	2 mL
Granulated sugar	1/2 tsp.	2 mL
Garlic powder	1/8 tsp.	0.5 mL
Cooking oil	2/3 cup	150 mL
Blue cheese, crumbled	1/4 cup	60 mL
SALAD		
Head of iceberg lettuce, shredded	1	1
Watercress, stems removed, chopped	1 cup	250 mL
Large hard-cooked eggs, divided	3	3
Green onions, sliced	4	4
Bacon slices, cooked and crumbled	8	8
Cooked chicken, cubed	2 1/2 cups	600 mL
Large tomato, finely chopped	1	1
Avocado, diced	1	1

Dressing: Combine all 8 ingredients in bowl. Mix well.

Salad: Combine lettuce and watercress in large salad bowl. Add about 1/4 dressing. Toss to coat.

Remove yolks and grate. Also grate whites separately. Arrange yolks in centre of bowl, and surround with whites. Make separate wedges of onions, bacon, chicken, tomato and avocado or mix these five together and pile around egg centre. Serve with rest of dressing. Serves 4 to 6.

***1 serving:** 600 Calories; 50 g Total Fat (27 g Mono, 11 g Poly, 8 g Sat); 200 mg Cholesterol; 11 g Carbohydrate; 5 g Fibre; 30 g Protein; 810 mg Sodium*

Note: You may prefer to make a wedge of crumbled blue cheese rather than add it to the dressing. You could also serve the lettuce on the side.

Salads.
First published in June 1984.

Oil
Vinegar

Spinach Cranberry Salad

This salad can be on the table in no time! Toasted nuts and dried berries add a delicious boost to greens and juicy oranges. The brilliant colours say "healthy and fresh."

Bag of fresh spinach	**6 oz.**	**170 g**
Pecan halves, toasted (see Tip, page 58)	**1/2 cup**	**125 mL**
Orange-flavoured dried cranberries	**1/4 cup**	**60 mL**
Medium oranges	**3**	**3**

Put first 3 ingredients into large bowl. Toss.

Squeeze juice from 1 orange. Set aside. Peel remaining 2 oranges. Cut oranges crosswise into 1/4 inch (6 mm) slices. Cut slices in half. Add to spinach mixture. Drizzle with juice. Sprinkle with salt and pepper. Toss gently. Makes about 6 1/2 cups (1.6 L). Serves 4.

1 serving: *165 Calories; 10 g Total Fat (6 g Mono, 2.5 g Poly, 0.8 g Sat); 0 mg Cholesterol; 19 g Carbohydrate; 5 g Fibre; 3 g Protein; 34 mg Sodium*

4-Ingredient Recipes.
First published in May 2006.

French Onion Soup

Even made from scratch, this soup is quick. Very appetizing.

Medium Spanish onions	4	4
Butter (or hard margarine)	1/4 cup	60 mL
Beef bouillon powder	2 tbsp.	30 mL
Water	6 cups	1.5 L
Salt	1 1/2 tsp.	7 mL
French bread slices, toasted (or croutons)	6	6
Grated mozzarella cheese	2 cups	500 mL

Cut peeled onions in half lengthwise. Slice into thin slices. Cut any long slices in half. Sauté in butter in frying pan until a rich brown colour. This is easier to do in batches.

Combine beef bouillon powder, water and salt in large pot. Heat. Stir. Add browned onion. Simmer to distribute flavour and to finish cooking onion. Ladle into 6 bowls.

Top with toasted slices of French bread or croutons. Cover with lots of cheese. Bake in 450°F (230°C) oven or broil to melt and brown cheese. If bowls aren't ovenproof, broil cheese-covered toast separately and place on soup to serve. Serves 6.

1 serving: *270 Calories; 16 g Total Fat (4.5 g Mono, 0.5 g Poly, 10 g Sat); 50 mg Cholesterol; 21 g Carbohydrate; 2 g Fibre; 11 g Protein; 1890 mg Sodium*

Variation: Substitute red onions for the white. Makes a delicious change in flavour.

Soups & Sandwiches.
First published in April 1987.

Spicy Yam Soup

A lovely, autumn soup with sweet yam and corn, and just a hint of heat. Just as good using sweet potato.

Butter (or hard margarine)	**2 tbsp.**	**30 mL**
Thinly sliced onion	**2 cups**	**500 mL**
Garlic cloves, minced	**4**	**4**
Paprika	**2 tsp.**	**10 mL**
Ground coriander	**1 tsp.**	**5 mL**
Cayenne pepper	**1/4–1/2 tsp.**	**1–2 mL**
Yams, peeled and cut into 1 1/2 inch (3.8 cm) cubes (about 5 cups, 1.25 L)	**2 lbs.**	**900 g**
Prepared chicken broth	**8 cups**	**2 L**
Can of cream-style corn	**14 oz.**	**398 mL**
Pepper, sprinkle		
Sour cream, for garnish	**1/4 cup**	**60 mL**
Chopped fresh chives, for garnish	**1/4 cup**	**60 mL**

Melt butter in large pot or Dutch oven on medium. Add onion. Cook, uncovered, for 5 to 10 minutes, stirring often, until softened.

Add next 4 ingredients. Heat and stir for 1 to 2 minutes until fragrant.

Add yam. Toss until coated.

Add broth. Stir. Bring to a boil. Reduce heat to medium-low. Cover. Simmer for 25 to 30 minutes, stirring occasionally, until yam is tender. Remove from heat. Let stand for 5 minutes. Process yam mixture, in 2 batches, in blender or food processor until smooth. Return to same pot.

Add corn and pepper. Stir. Bring to a boil on medium-high. Heat and stir for 3 to 4 minutes until heated through.

Ladle soup into 8 individual bowls. Swirl a dollop of sour cream through centre of each. Sprinkle chives over top. Makes 8 cups (2 L).

1 cup (250 mL): *243 Calories; 5 g Total Fat (2.6 g Mono, 0.8 g Poly, 1.1 g Sat); 0 mg Cholesterol; 43 g Carbohydrate; 6 g Fibre; 8 g Protein; 1018 mg Sodium*

Herbs & Spices.
First published in August 2004.

Lemon Lentil Soup

A fragrant soup with tangy, creamy broth. A feast for the eyes as well as the palate.

Cooking oil	**1 tbsp.**	**15 mL**
Chopped onion	**1 1/2 cups**	**375 mL**
Chopped carrot	**1 1/2 cups**	**375 mL**
Curry powder	**1 1/2 tbsp.**	**25 mL**
Prepared vegetable (or chicken) broth	**6 cups**	**1.5 L**
Can of lentils, rinsed and drained	**19 oz.**	**540 mL**
Can of coconut milk	**14 oz.**	**398 mL**
Bay leaves	**2**	**2**
Fresh spinach leaves, lightly packed	**2 cups**	**500 mL**
Lemon juice	**2 tbsp.**	**30 mL**
Salt	**1/4 tsp.**	**1 mL**

Heat cooking oil in large pot or Dutch oven on medium-high. Add onion and carrot. Cook for about 5 minutes, stirring often, until onion starts to soften.

Add curry powder. Heat and stir for 1 to 2 minutes until fragrant.

Add next 4 ingredients. Stir. Bring to a boil. Reduce heat to medium. Cover. Simmer for about 5 minutes, stirring occasionally, until carrot is tender. Discard bay leaves.

Add remaining 3 ingredients. Heat and stir for about 2 minutes until spinach is wilted. Makes about 11 cups (2.75 L).

***1 cup (250 mL):** 156 Calories; 9.8 g Total Fat (1.4 g Mono, 0.7 g Poly, 6.9 g Sat); 0 mg Cholesterol; 12 g Carbohydrate; 3 g Fibre; 7 g Protein; 592 mg Sodium*

Make It A Meal with pappadum (a wafer-thin Indian bread made with lentil flour), heated according to package directions. If desired, top pappadum with tomato salsa made with chopped tomato, cucumber and fresh mint. Drizzle with small amounts of lemon juice and olive oil and sprinkle with salt and pepper.

30-Minute Weekday Meals.
First published in May 2005.

BBQ Party Salad

Invite guests early and have them cut and chop while you barbecue. Great summer salad.

Dijon mustard	2 tbsp.	30 mL
Freshly ground pepper	1 tsp.	5 mL
Sirloin steak, 1 1/2 inch (3.8 cm) thick, blotted dry	2 lbs.	900 g
Ears of corn, husked	2	2
Olive (or cooking) oil	1 1/2 tbsp.	25 mL
Green, red or yellow peppers, halved and seeded	3	3
Medium zucchini, with peel, sliced in half lengthwise	2	2
Red onions, sliced into 1/4 inch (6 mm) rings	2	2
Olive (or cooking) oil	2 tbsp.	30 mL
Tomatoes, diced	2	2
Sliced ripe pitted olives	1/2 cup	125 mL
DRESSING		
Balsamic (or red wine) vinegar	3 tbsp.	45 mL
Garlic cloves, minced (or 1/2 tsp., 2 mL, powder)	2	2
Salt	1 1/2 tsp.	7 mL
Pepper	1/2 tsp.	2 mL
Olive (or cooking) oil	1/3 cup	75 mL
Chopped fresh parsley (or 2 1/2 tsp., 12 mL, flakes)	3 tbsp.	45 mL
Chopped chives (or green onion)	3 tbsp.	45 mL
Chopped mixed salad greens	4 cups	1 L

Combine mustard and pepper in small bowl. Spread on both sides of steak. Barbecue over medium-high heat for 8 to 10 minutes per side until desired doneness. Cover with foil. Set aside.

(continued on next page)

The Beef Book.
First published in February 2002.

Brush corn with first amount of olive oil. Barbecue over medium heat, turning until kernels start to crackle and are lightly golden. Cool slightly. Cut kernels off cob with sharp knife. Place in very large bowl.

Brush peppers, zucchini and onion rings with second amount of olive oil. Barbecue over medium heat until golden. Dice. Add to corn mixture. Stir.

Add tomato and olives.

Dressing: Combine vinegar, garlic, salt and pepper. Whisk in olive oil. Add parsley and chives. Toss with corn mixture. Remove steak from foil. Cut steak diagonally across grain into thin slices. Slice crosswise into 1 inch (2.5 cm) strips. Add to corn mixture. Toss.

Add salad greens. Toss to mix. Serves 8.

***1 serving:** 460 Calories; 34 g Total Fat (20 g Mono, 2.5 g Poly, 2.5 g Sat); 80 mg Cholesterol; 15 g Carbohydrate; 3 g Fibre; 26 g Protein; 650 mg Sodium*

Strawberry Pork Salad

Grilled pork is at its best when tossed with fresh greens and sweet strawberries. Walnuts and goat cheese add richness and round out the flavours of this delicious, eye-catching salad.

Pork tenderloin, trimmed of fat	**3/4 lb.**	**340 g**
Salt	**1/4 tsp.**	**1 mL**
Pepper	**1/8 tsp.**	**0.5 mL**
Olive (or cooking) oil	**3 tbsp.**	**45 mL**
Strawberry jam, warmed	**3 tbsp.**	**45 mL**
White balsamic (or white wine) vinegar	**2 tbsp.**	**30 mL**
Coarsely ground pepper	**1/4 tsp.**	**1 mL**
Spring mix lettuce, lightly packed	**8 cups**	**2 L**
Sliced fresh strawberries	**2/3 cup**	**150 mL**
Walnut pieces, toasted (see Tip, page 58)	**1/2 cup**	**125 mL**
Thinly sliced celery	**1/3 cup**	**75 mL**
Thinly sliced sweet onion	**1/3 cup**	**75 mL**
Goat (chèvre) cheese, cut up	**3 oz.**	**85 g**

Preheat gas barbecue to medium (see Note). Sprinkle tenderloin with salt and pepper. Cook on greased grill for about 20 minutes, turning once, until internal temperature reaches 155°F (68°C). Transfer to cutting board. Cover with foil. Let stand for 20 minutes. Internal temperature should rise to at least 160°F (71°C). Slice thinly.

Whisk next 4 ingredients in small bowl.

Toss remaining 6 ingredients and pork in extra-large bowl. Drizzle with olive oil mixture. Toss. Makes about 10 cups (2.5 L).

1 1/2 cups (375 mL): *249 Calories; 16.7 g Total Fat (6.7 g Mono, 5.4 g Poly, 3.9 g Sat); 39 mg Cholesterol; 11 g Carbohydrate; 2 g Fibre; 15 g Protein; 172 mg Sodium*

Note: Too cold to barbecue? Use the oven instead! Cook tenderloin in 475°F (240°C) oven for 25 to 30 minutes until internal temperature reaches 155°F (68°C). Transfer to cutting board. Cover with foil. Let stand for 20 minutes. Internal temperature should rise to at least 160°F (71°C).

Meal Salads.
First published in April 2010.

Thai-Style Pork Soup

Spicy curry heats up this hearty soup. It makes a great starter for an Asian meal.

Cooking oil	**1 tbsp.**	**15 mL**
Pork tenderloin, trimmed of fat and cut into thin strips (see Tip, below)	**1/2 lb.**	**225 g**
Red curry paste	**1 tbsp.**	**15 mL**
Low-sodium prepared chicken broth	**4 cups**	**1 L**
Can of cut baby corn, drained	**14 oz.**	**398 mL**
Thinly sliced red pepper	**1 cup**	**250 mL**
Fish sauce	**1 tsp.**	**5 mL**
Brown sugar, packed	**1 tsp.**	**5 mL**
Fresh spinach, stems removed, lightly packed	**2 cups**	**500 mL**
Finely shredded basil (or 1 1/2 tsp., 7 mL, dried)	**2 tbsp.**	**30 mL**
Lime juice	**1 tbsp.**	**15 mL**

Heat cooking oil in large pot or Dutch oven on medium-high. Add pork. Cook for about 5 minutes, stirring occasionally, until browned. Transfer to small bowl. Cover to keep warm.

Heat and stir curry paste in same large pot on medium for about 1 minute until fragrant.

Add next 5 ingredients. Stir. Bring to a boil on medium-high. Reduce heat to medium-low. Cover. Simmer for about 5 minutes until red pepper is softened.

Add pork and spinach. Stir. Simmer for about 2 minutes, stirring occasionally, until pork is heated through and spinach is wilted.

Add basil and lime juice. Stir. Serves 4.

1 serving: *199 Calories; 7.7 g Total Fat (3.9 g Mono, 1.8 g Poly, 1.2 g Sat); 35 mg Cholesterol; 17 g Carbohydrate; 3 g Fibre; 18 g Protein; 907 mg Sodium*

Easy Healthy Recipes.
First published in January 2010.

TIP

To slice meat easily, freeze for about 30 minutes. If using frozen, partially thaw before slicing.

Vegetable Tortellini Bowl

Tortellini turns this light tomato broth packed with vegetables into a meal.

Cooking oil	1 tbsp.	15 mL
Chopped onion	2 cups	500 mL
Garlic cloves, minced (or 1/2 tsp., 2 mL, powder)	2	2
Chicken stock	12 cups	3 L
Can of diced tomatoes, drained	14 oz.	398 mL
Grated carrot	1 1/2 cups	375 mL
Chopped zucchini (with peel)	1 1/2 cups	375 mL
Chopped yellow or red pepper	1 cup	250 mL
Bay leaves	2	2
Dried rosemary, crushed	1 tsp.	5 mL
Salt	1/4 tsp.	1 mL
Package of fresh beef-filled tortellini	12 1/2 oz.	350 g
Fresh spinach leaves, lightly packed	3 cups	750 mL

Heat cooking oil in Dutch oven or large pot on medium-high. Add onion and garlic. Cook for 5 to 10 minutes, stirring often, until onion is softened.

Add next 8 ingredients. Stir. Bring to a boil.

Add tortellini. Stir. Reduce heat to medium. Boil gently, uncovered, for about 8 minutes, stirring occasionally, until tortellini is tender but firm.

Add spinach. Stir. Cook for about 2 minutes until spinach is wilted. Discard bay leaves. Makes about 15 cups (3.75 L). Serves 8.

***1 serving:** 235 Calories; 6.8 g Total Fat (1.1 g Mono, 0.7 g Poly, 0.9 g Sat); 15 mg Cholesterol; 36 g Carbohydrate; 3 g Fibre; 10 g Protein; 1602 mg Sodium*

Soups.
First published in October 2006.

Rouladen

When cutting into these rolls, you'll find dill pickle as well as onion and bacon.

Pieces of thinly sliced beef round steak	**8**	**8**
Salt, sprinkle		
Pepper, sprinkle		
Bacon slices, halved crosswise	**8**	**8**
Large onions, halved and sliced	**1–2**	**1–2**
Medium green peppers, cut into strips	**1–2**	**1–2**
Large dill pickles, quartered lengthwise	**2**	**2**
All-purpose flour for coating	**1/4 cup**	**60 mL**
Hard margarine (butter browns too fast)	**2 tbsp.**	**30 mL**
Butter (or hard margarine)	**6 tbsp.**	**90 mL**
All-purpose flour	**6 tbsp.**	**90 mL**
Beef bouillon powder	**2 tbsp.**	**30 mL**
Water	**4 cups**	**1 L**
Ketchup	**1/4 cup**	**60 mL**

Lay meat slices on flat surface. Sprinkle with salt and pepper. Lay 2 pieces of bacon on top of meat followed by onion, green pepper and a slice of dill pickle. Roll up each steak and tie with string.

Coat rolls with flour. Brown in margarine in frying pan. Add more margarine if needed. Place rolls in small roaster.

Melt butter in frying pan. Mix in second amount of flour and bouillon powder. Stir in water and ketchup until it boils and thickens. Pour over meat in roaster. Cover. Bake in 350°F (175°C) oven until fork tender, about 1 1/2 to 2 hours. Makes 8 servings.

1 serving: *450 Calories; 33 g Total Fat (13 g Mono, 3.5 g Poly, 13 g Sat); 95 mg Cholesterol; 14 g Carbohydrate; less than 1 g Fibre; 23 g Protein; 1350 mg Sodium*

Dinners Of The World.
First published in September 1991.

Lasagne

Lasagne needn't be a winter food. It won't heat up the kitchen when you use your microwave.

Lasagne noodles	8	8
Water to cover		
Cooking oil	1 tbsp.	15 mL
MEAT SAUCE		
Lean ground beef	1 lb.	454 g
Chopped onion	1/4 cup	60 mL
Cans of tomato sauce	2 x 7 1/2 oz.	2 x 213 mL
Can of tomato paste	5 1/2 oz.	156 mL
Dried oregano	1 tsp.	5 mL
Dried basil	1 tsp.	5 mL
Garlic salt	1 tsp.	5 mL
Granulated sugar	2 tsp.	10 mL
CHEESE MIXTURE		
1% cottage cheese	2 cups	500 mL
Large egg	1	1
Grated Parmesan cheese	1/2 cup	125 mL
Parsley flakes	2 tsp.	10 mL
Salt	1 tsp.	5 mL
Pepper	1/8 tsp.	0.5 mL
Grated medium Cheddar cheese	1 cup	250 mL
Grated mozzarella cheese	1 cup	250 mL
Paprika, sprinkle		

Place noodles in lasagne dish. Add water to cover and cooking oil. Cook on high (100%) about 16 minutes until tender but firm. Drain.

Meat Sauce: Crumble beef with onion in 2 quart (2 L) bowl. Cover with waxed paper. Cook on high (100%) for about 3 minutes. Stir. Cook on high (100%) for about 4 minutes more until no pink remains in beef. Drain off fat.

Add next 6 ingredients to beef mixture. Cover. Cook on high (100%) for about 6 minutes. Stir.

(continued on next page)

Microwave Cooking.
First published in September 1993.

Cheese Mixture: Stir first 6 ingredients together in small bowl.

To assemble, layer in 9 x 13 inch (23 x 33 cm) glass pan (see Note) as follows:

1. A bit of meat sauce to cover bottom
2. Layer of noodles
3. 1/2 of meat sauce
4. Cheese mixture
5. Layer of noodles
6. 1/2 of meat sauce
7. Cheddar cheese
8. Mozzarella cheese
9. Paprika sprinkle

Cover with plastic wrap, venting corner. Cook on medium (50%) for about 25 minutes, rotating dish 1/2 turn at half-time if you don't have a turntable. Let stand, uncovered, for 10 minutes. Cuts into 8 squares.

1 square: *440 Calories; 21 g Total Fat (8 g Mono, 1 g Poly, 10 g Sat); 95 mg Cholesterol; 26 g Carbohydrate; 3 g Fibre; 32 g Protein; 1420 mg Sodium*

Note: If you have a turntable, be sure dish will turn. If it won't, assemble in large casserole.

Teener's Dish

Pasta is added raw to this casserole—a real time saver in preparation.

Lean ground beef	1 lb.	454 g
Chopped onion	1 cup	250 mL
Green pepper, seeded and slivered	1	1
Frozen kernel corn	1 1/2 cups	375 mL
Salt	3/4 tsp.	4 mL
Pepper	1/4 tsp.	1 mL
Dry coloured fusilli (or other pasta)	2 2/3 cups	650 mL
Tomato juice	2 3/4 cups	675 mL
Grated light sharp Cheddar cheese	1 cup	250 mL

Spray frying pan with no-stick cooking spray. Add ground beef, onion and green pepper. Sauté until no pink remains in beef and onion is soft.

Add corn, salt and pepper. Stir.

Layer 1/2 dry fusilli in 3 quart (3 L) casserole followed by 1/2 beef mixture, second 1/2 fusilli and second 1/2 beef.

Pour tomato juice over all. Cover. Bake in 350°F (175°C) oven for 50 to 60 minutes until noodles are tender.

Sprinkle with cheese. Bake, uncovered, for 5 minutes more. Makes 6 2/3 cups (1.5 L).

1 cup (250 mL): *460 Calories; 14 g Total Fat (4.5 g Mono, 0 g Poly, 6 g Sat); 55 mg Cholesterol; 51 g Carbohydrate; 4 g Fibre; 26 g Protein; 750 mg Sodium*

Light Casseroles.
First published in September 1994.

Oven Beef Stew

Your meal-in-one waiting in the oven.

Stewing beef, trimmed of fat, cut bite size	**1/2 lb.**	**225 g**
Medium-small potatoes, cut bite size	**2**	**2**
Medium carrots, cut bite size	**2**	**2**
Medium onion, cut bite size	**1**	**1**
Sliced celery	**1/2 cup**	**125 mL**
Can of diced tomatoes, with juice	**14 oz.**	**398 mL**
Granulated sugar	**2 tsp.**	**10 mL**
Beef bouillon powder	**2 tsp.**	**10 mL**
Prepared horseradish	**1 tsp.**	**5 mL**
Salt	**1/2 tsp.**	**2 mL**
Pepper	**1/8 tsp.**	**0.5 mL**
Water	**1/3 cup**	**75 mL**

Place beef in ungreased 2 quart (2 L) casserole or small roaster. Add vegetables.

Combine remaining 7 ingredients in bowl. Stir well. Pour over beef. Cover. Bake in 300°F (150°C) oven for about 3 1/4 to 3 1/2 hours until beef is very tender. Makes 4 1/2 cups (1.1 L). Serves 2.

1 serving: *460 Calories; 9 g Total Fat (3 g Mono, 0.5 g Poly, 3 g Sat); 55 mg Cholesterol; 65 g Carbohydrate; 7 g Fibre; 33 g Protein; 2310 mg Sodium*

Cooking For Two.
First published in September 1997.

Beef and Mushroom Pizza

Pass the grated Parmesan cheese to sprinkle over this moist pizza.

BASIC PIZZA CRUST		
All-purpose flour	**2 cups**	**500 mL**
Instant yeast	**1 1/4 tsp.**	**6 mL**
Salt	**1/4 tsp.**	**1 mL**
Warm water	**2/3 cup**	**150 mL**
Cooking oil	**2 tbsp.**	**30 mL**
TOPPING		
Lean ground beef	**3/4 lb.**	**340 g**
Pizza sauce	**1/2 cup**	**125 mL**
Grated part-skim mozzarella cheese	**3/4 cup**	**175 mL**
Sliced fresh mushrooms	**1 3/4 cups**	**425 mL**
Grated part-skim mozzarella cheese	**3/4 cup**	**175 mL**
Paprika, sprinkle		

Basic Pizza Crust: Put first 3 ingredients into medium bowl. Stir together well.

Add warm water and cooking oil. Mix well until dough leaves sides of bowl. Knead on lightly floured surface for 5 to 8 minutes until smooth and elastic.

At this point you may choose to roll out and press in greased 12 inch (30 cm) pizza pan, forming rim around edge. Or place dough in large greased bowl, turning once to grease top. Cover with tea towel. Let stand in oven with light on and door closed for about 1 hour until doubled in size. Punch dough down. Roll out and press in greased 12 inch (30 cm) pizza pan, forming rim around edge.

Topping: Scramble-fry ground beef in medium non-stick frying pan. Drain.

Spread sauce over crust. Distribute beef over sauce. Sprinkle with first amount of cheese.

(continued on next page)

Pizza!
First published in April 1999.

Cover pizza with mushrooms. Sprinkle second amount of cheese over all. Sprinkle with paprika. Bake on bottom rack in 425°F (220°C) oven for about 15 minutes, or for about 10 minutes if using partially baked crust. Cuts into 8 wedges.

1 wedge: *340 Calories; 15 g Total Fat (6 g Mono, 1.5 g Poly, 5 g Sat); 45 mg Cholesterol; 26 g Carbohydrate; 1 g Fibre; 19 g Protein; 330 mg Sodium*

Porcupine Meatball Stew

An old recipe that always satisfies. This dish has a long cooking time but takes only 30 minutes to prepare. Garnish with parsley.

Extra-lean ground beef	1 lb.	454 g
Finely chopped onion	1/4 cup	60 mL
Garlic clove, minced (or 1/4 tsp., 1 mL, powder)	1	1
Large egg	1	1
Fine dry bread crumbs	1/3 cup	75 mL
Seasoned salt	1 tsp.	5 mL
Pepper	1/8 tsp.	0.5 mL
Long-grain white rice, uncooked	1/4 cup	60 mL
Small onion, cut into wedges	1	1
Sliced carrot	2 1/4 cups	550 mL
Medium potatoes, cut into chunks	2	2
Diced green pepper	1/2 cup	125 mL
Can of stewed tomatoes, with juice	14 oz.	398 mL
Water	1/2 cup	125 mL
Beef bouillon powder	1 tsp.	5 mL

Combine first 8 ingredients in medium bowl. Divide and shape into 12 meatballs. Arrange in single layer in bottom of ungreased 2 quart (2 L) casserole.

Layer next 4 ingredients, in order given, over meatballs.

Heat tomatoes with juice, water and bouillon powder in small saucepan until boiling. Pour over vegetables. Cover. Bake in 325°F (160°C) oven for 2 hours. Makes 6 cups (1.5 L).

1 cup (250 mL): *290 Calories; 7 g Total Fat (3 g Mono, 0.5 g Poly, 3 g Sat); 75 mg Cholesterol; 35 g Carbohydrate; 4 g Fibre; 21 g Protein; 770 mg Sodium*

Stews, Chilies & Chowders.
First published in October 2001.

Hunt's

Ground Beef Curry

There's lots of colour in this flavourful, mild curry. If you've never used chili paste before, here's a good place to start. If you're already a fan, add as much as you like.

Cooking oil	**1 tsp.**	**5 mL**
Lean ground beef	**1 lb.**	**454 g**
Chopped onion	**1 cup**	**250 mL**
Garlic clove, minced (or 1/4 tsp., 1 mL, powder)	**1**	**1**
All-purpose flour	**2 tbsp.**	**30 mL**
Curry powder	**2 tbsp.**	**30 mL**
Prepared beef broth	**1 1/2 cups**	**375 mL**
Tomato juice	**1 1/4 cups**	**300 mL**
Can of chickpeas (garbanzo beans), rinsed and drained	**14 oz.**	**398 mL**
Diced tomato	**1 1/2 cups**	**375 mL**
Frozen peas, thawed	**1 cup**	**250 mL**
Salt	**1/4 tsp.**	**1 mL**
Chili paste (sambal oelek), optional	**1/2–1 tsp.**	**2–5 mL**
Plain yogurt	**1/2 cup**	**125 mL**
Chopped fresh cilantro or parsley, for garnish		

Heat cooking oil in large frying pan on medium. Add ground beef and onion. Scramble-fry for about 10 minutes until beef is no longer pink. Drain.

Add garlic. Heat and stir for 1 to 2 minutes until fragrant.

Add flour and curry powder. Heat and stir for 1 minute.

Slowly add broth, stirring constantly. Add tomato juice and chickpeas. Stir until boiling. Boil gently, uncovered, for about 15 minutes, stirring occasionally, until thickened.

(continued on next page)

Ground Beef Recipes.
First published in February 2006.

Add next 4 ingredients. Stir. Cook for about 5 minutes, stirring occasionally, until peas are heated through. Remove from heat.

Add yogurt. Stir well. Remove to large serving bowl.

Garnish with cilantro. Serves 6.

***1 serving:** 262 Calories; 9.2 g Total Fat (3.7 g Mono, 1 g Poly, 3 g Sat); 39 mg Cholesterol; 24 g Carbohydrate; 4 g Fibre; 21 g Protein; 671 mg Sodium*

Coq Au Vin

Wine flavour is evident in this dish that is served in fine restaurants but is easy to make at home.

Pearl onions, peeled (see Note)	36	36
Whole chicken, divided into parts, skin removed	3 lbs.	1.4 kg
Bacon slices, cooked crisp and crumbled	6	6
Small fresh mushrooms	2 cups	500 mL
Thinly sliced celery	1/2 cup	125 mL
Beef bouillon powder	2 tsp.	10 mL
Warm water	1 1/2 cups	375 mL
Salt	1/2 tsp.	2 mL
Pepper	1/4 tsp.	1 mL
Garlic powder	1/4 tsp.	1 mL
Parsley flakes	1 tsp.	5 mL
Ground thyme	1/4 tsp.	1 mL
Bay leaf	1	1
Dry (or alcohol-free) red wine	2 cups	500 mL
GRAVY		
All-purpose flour	2 tbsp.	30 mL
Salt	1/4 tsp.	1 mL
Pepper, sprinkle		
Meat liquid, strained if needed, fat removed, plus water to make	1 cup	250 mL
Chopped fresh parsley, for garnish		

Place onion in 5 quart (5 L) slow cooker. Arrange chicken pieces, bacon, mushrooms and celery in order given over top.

Stir bouillon powder and warm water together in small bowl. Add salt, pepper, garlic powder, parsley flakes, thyme and bay leaf. Stir. Pour over chicken.

Add wine. Cover. Cook on Low for 8 to 10 hours or on High for 4 to 5 hours. Discard bay leaf. Transfer chicken mixture to serving dish.

(continued on next page)

Slow Cooker Recipes.
First published in September 1998.

Gravy: Make gravy with remaining liquid. Combine flour, salt and pepper in saucepan. Stir.

Gradually whisk in meat liquid and water until no lumps remain. Heat and stir until boiling and thickened. Pour over chicken mixture.

Garnish with parsley. Serves 6.

1 serving: *420 Calories; 10 g Total Fat (3.5 g Mono, 2 g Poly, 2.5 g Sat); 155 mg Cholesterol; 15 g Carbohydrate; less than 1 g Fibre; 52 g Protein; 1120 mg Sodium*

Note: To peel pearl onions easily, blanch in boiling water for about 2 minutes. Rinse in cold water and simply peel away skin.

Elegant Chicken

Incredibly good. The sauce does it.

All-purpose flour	2 tbsp.	30 mL
Salt	1/8 tsp.	0.5 mL
Pepper, just a pinch		
Paprika	1/8 tsp.	0.5 mL
Hard margarine (butter browns too fast)	1 tbsp.	15 mL
Boneless, skinless chicken breast halves (4–6 oz., 113–170 g, each)	4	4
HAZELNUT SAUCE		
Sliced fresh mushrooms	1 cup	250 mL
Dry (or alcohol-free) white wine	1/2 cup	125 mL
Can of condensed cream of mushroom soup	1/2 x 10 oz.	1/2 x 284 mL
Garlic powder	1/4 tsp.	1 mL
Flaked hazelnuts (filberts), toasted (see Tip, page 58)	2 tbsp.	30 mL

Combine flour, salt, pepper and paprika in saucer. Mix. Place in paper bag.

Melt margarine in frying pan. Coat chicken with flour mixture, shaking 2 or 3 pieces at a time in bag. Cook and brown chicken until no pink remains. Remove to serving bowl. Keep warm.

Hazelnut Sauce: In same frying pan add mushrooms and wine. Stir to loosen brown bits. Boil gently for 3 to 4 minutes to soften mushrooms and reduce liquid.

Stir in soup, garlic powder and hazelnuts. Return to a boil. Pour over chicken. Makes 4 servings.

***1 serving:** 250 Calories; 9 g Total Fat (3.5 g Mono, 2 g Poly, 1.5 g Sat); 65 mg Cholesterol; 8 g Carbohydrate; less than 1 g Fibre; 28 g Protein; 430 mg Sodium*

Chicken, Etc.
First published in April 1995.

Tortellini

These little gems are served in a creamy sauce. For a spicier dish, serve with a tomato sauce.

FILLING		
Finely chopped cooked chicken	1 cup	250 mL
Grated Parmesan cheese	3 tbsp.	45 mL
Large egg	1	1
Salt	1/4 tsp.	1 mL
Pepper, sprinkle		
TORTELLINI		
All-purpose flour	2 cups	500 mL
Large eggs	4	4
Salt	1/2 tsp.	2 mL
Boiling water	4 qts.	4 L
PARMESAN SAUCE		
Whipping cream	1 cup	250 mL
Butter (or hard margarine)	1 tbsp.	15 mL
Grated Parmesan cheese	2/3 cup	150 mL
Chopped parsley	1/4 cup	60 mL
Salt	1/8 tsp.	0.5 mL

Filling: Mix all 5 ingredients together well. Add a bit of water if needed to hold together.

Tortellini: Mix flour, eggs and salt together well to form a stiff dough. Divide into 4 balls. Roll on lightly floured surface. Cut into 2 inch (5 cm) circles. Place 1/4 tsp. (1 mL) filling on each. Moisten edges with water, fold over, press to seal. Pull ends together away from curved sides. Use a touch of water to seal.

Cook uncovered in large pot of boiling water 8 to 10 minutes until tender. Makes about 4 dozen.

Parmesan Sauce: Mix all 5 ingredients together in saucepan. Bring to a slow simmer. Pour over tortellini. Serves 2.

1 serving: *1200 Calories; 62 g Total Fat (18 g Mono, 3.5 g Poly, 36 g Sat); 245 mg Cholesterol; 102 g Carbohydrate; 4 g Fibre; 59 g Protein; 1950 mg Sodium*

Pasta.
First published in April 1990.

Smoky Chicken Penne

Smokin'! This spicy chicken penne has a double-dose of smoky flavour from bacon and chipotle peppers.

Bacon slices, diced	**4**	**4**
Lean ground chicken	**1 lb.**	**454 g**
Chopped onion	**1/2 cup**	**125 mL**
Garlic clove, minced (or 1/4 tsp., 1 mL, powder)	**1**	**1**
Italian seasoning	**1 tsp.**	**5 mL**
Pasta sauce	**4 cups**	**1 L**
Penne pasta	**4 cups**	**1 L**
Water	**4 cups**	**1 L**
Finely chopped chipotle peppers in adobo sauce (see Tip, below)	**1/2 tsp.**	**2 mL**
Diced green pepper	**1 cup**	**250 mL**
Grated mozzarella cheese (optional)	**1/2 cup**	**125 mL**

Cook bacon in Dutch oven on medium-high, stirring occasionally, until starting to crisp. Add chicken. Scramble-fry for about 5 minutes until chicken is no longer pink.

Add next 3 ingredients. Stir. Cook, uncovered, for about 3 minutes, stirring occasionally, until onion starts to soften.

Add next 4 ingredients. Stir. Bring to a boil, stirring often. Reduce heat to medium-low. Simmer, covered, for about 15 minutes, stirring often, until pasta is almost tender.

(continued on next page)

Perfect Pasta And Sauces.
First published in August 2008.

TIP

Chipotle chili peppers are smoked jalapeno peppers. Be sure to wash your hands after handling. To store any leftover chipotle chili peppers, divide into recipe-friendly portions and freeze, with sauce, in airtight containers for up to 1 year.

Add green pepper. Stir. Cook, covered, for about 5 minutes until pasta is tender but firm and pepper is tender-crisp.

Sprinkle with cheese. Makes about 9 1/2 cups (2.4 L).

1 cup (250 mL): *336 Calories; 9.4 g Total Fat (1.9 g Mono, 0.5 g Poly, 2.5 g Sat); 38 mg Cholesterol; 48 g Carbohydrate; 2 g Fibre; 17 g Protein; 378 mg Sodium*

Chicken Chow Mein

The dark-coloured sauce coats the chicken and vegetables nicely.

Can of condensed chicken broth	10 oz.	284 mL
Cornstarch	2 tbsp.	30 mL
Fancy (mild) molasses	2 tbsp.	30 mL
Low-sodium soy sauce	3 tbsp.	45 mL
Short-grain white rice	1 1/4 cups	300 mL
Water	2 1/2 cups	625 mL
Salt	1/2 tsp.	2 mL
Cooking oil	1 tbsp.	15 mL
Boneless, skinless chicken breast halves (about 3), cut into thin strips	3/4 lb.	340 g
Cooking oil	1 tsp.	5 mL
Small green pepper, cut into slivers	1	1
Chopped onion	1 cup	250 mL
Chopped celery	1/2 cup	125 mL
Fresh bean sprouts	2 cups	500 mL
Can of sliced water chestnuts, drained	8 oz.	227 mL
Can of bamboo shoots, drained	8 oz.	227 mL
Can of sliced mushrooms, drained	10 oz.	284 mL
Dry chow mein noodles	1 cup	250 mL

Stir chicken broth into cornstarch in small bowl. Add molasses and soy sauce. Stir. Set aside.

Cook rice in water and salt in large covered saucepan for 15 to 20 minutes until tender and water is absorbed. Remove from heat. Cover to keep warm.

Heat wok or frying pan on medium-high. Add first amount of cooking oil. Add chicken strips. Stir-fry for 4 to 5 minutes until no pink remains in chicken. Transfer to bowl.

(continued on next page)

Stir-Fry.
First published in March 2000.

Add second amount of cooking oil to hot wok. Add green pepper, onion and celery. Stir-fry for 3 to 5 minutes until soft.

Add bean sprouts. Stir-fry for 1 minute.

Add water chestnuts, bamboo shoots and mushrooms. Stir-fry until hot. Add chicken. Stir cornstarch mixture. Stir into chicken mixture until boiling and thickened. Serve over rice. Sprinkle with noodles. Serves 4.

1 serving: *580 Calories; 10 g Total Fat (3 g Mono, 2 g Poly, 2 g Sat); 50 mg Cholesterol; 92 g Carbohydrate; 7 g Fibre; 31 g Protein; 1740 mg Sodium*

Honey Garlic Crostata

Sweet and saucy chicken and vegetables crowned with golden puff pastry.

Liquid honey	**1/4 cup**	**60 mL**
Dry sherry	**2 tbsp.**	**30 mL**
Soy sauce	**2 tbsp.**	**30 mL**
Garlic cloves, minced	**4**	**4**
Dijon mustard	**1 tbsp.**	**15 mL**
Pepper	**1/2 tsp.**	**2 mL**
Sesame oil (optional)	**1 tsp.**	**5 mL**
Cooking oil	**2 tsp.**	**10 mL**
Boneless, skinless chicken breast halves, cut into 1 inch (2.5 cm) cubes	**1/2 lb.**	**225 g**
Cooking oil	**2 tsp.**	**10 mL**
Chopped onion	**1 cup**	**250 mL**
Chopped red pepper	**1 cup**	**250 mL**
Frozen mixed vegetables	**1 cup**	**250 mL**
Package of puff pastry (14 oz., 397 g), thawed according to package directions	**1/2**	**1/2**

Combine first 7 ingredients in small bowl. Set aside.

Heat first amount of cooking oil in large frying pan on medium-high. Add chicken. Cook for 2 to 3 minutes, stirring occasionally, until browned. Remove to plate. Reduce heat to medium.

Add second amount of cooking oil to same frying pan. Add onion and red pepper. Cook for 5 to 10 minutes, stirring often, until onion is golden. Add chicken and honey mixture. Stir. Cook for 3 minutes. Add frozen vegetables. Stir. Transfer to large bowl. Cool.

(continued on next page)

Chicken Now.
First published in May 2007.

Roll out puff pastry on lightly floured surface to 11 inch (28 cm) diameter circle. Place on baking sheet. Spoon chicken mixture onto centre of pastry, leaving 2 inch (5 cm) edge. Fold a section of edge up and over edge of filling. Repeat with next section, allowing pastry to overlap so that a fold is created. Repeat until pastry border is completely folded around filling. Bake in 375°F (190°C) oven for 25 to 30 minutes until pastry is puffed and golden. Let stand for 5 minutes before serving. Serves 4.

***1 serving:** 640 Calories; 32.2 g Total Fat (17.4 g Mono, 4.0 g Poly, 7.9 g Sat); 33 mg Cholesterol; 62 g Carbohydrate; 4 g Fibre; 22 g Protein; 1272 mg Sodium*

Stuffed Turkey Scaloppine

What a wonderful stuffing surprise inside! There is quite a difference in flavour (and cost) between the prosciutto and the ham. Pick your preference.

Lean prosciutto or cooked ham, chopped	4 oz.	113 g
Grated part-skim mozzarella cheese	1/2 cup	125 g
Garlic clove, minced	1	1
Chopped fresh parsley	1 tbsp.	15 mL
Chopped fresh basil	1 tbsp.	15 mL
Thin turkey scaloppine	1 lb.	454 g
Can of plum tomatoes, with juice	28 oz.	796 mL
Granulated sugar	1 tsp.	5 mL
Dried basil	1 tsp.	5 mL
Dried oregano	1/2 tsp.	2 mL
Pepper	1/4 tsp.	1 mL
Cornstarch	1 tbsp.	15 mL
Water	1 tbsp.	15 mL
Spaghetti	8 oz.	225 g
Boiling water	8 cups	2 L
Salt (optional)	1 tsp.	5 mL

Combine prosciutto, cheese, garlic, parsley and fresh basil in small bowl.

Pound out scaloppine with flat side of mallet until 1/4 inch (6 mm) thick. Divide into 8 serving size pieces. Place about 3 tbsp. (45 mL) prosciutto mixture on narrow end of each scaloppine. Roll up, tucking in sides. Hold closed with wooden picks or tie with butchers' string. Lightly grease large non-stick skillet. Brown rolls on all sides until golden.

Chop tomatoes coarsely and add, with juice, to skillet. Add sugar, dried basil, oregano and pepper. Cover. Simmer for 30 minutes. Remove rolls to plate. Keep warm.

(continued on next page)

Low-Fat Cooking.
First published in February 2001.

Mix cornstarch and water in small cup. Stir into tomato sauce to thicken slightly. Makes 3 cups (750 mL) sauce.

Cook pasta in boiling water and salt in large Dutch oven for 7 to 9 minutes until tender but firm. Drain. Rinse. Drain again. Arrange in large pasta bowl. Pour sauce over pasta and toss lightly. Serve with turkey rolls. Serves 8.

***1 serving:** 240 Calories; 3.5 g Total Fat (0 g Mono, 0 g Poly, 1.5 g Sat); 50 mg Cholesterol; 27 g Carbohydrate; 2 g Fibre; 24 g Protein; 550 mg Sodium*

Just for the Halibut

Grated Parmesan adds to the flavour of this crumbed and browned dish. The rich brown colour comes from dry onion soup. Very good.

Dry onion soup	**2 tbsp.**	**30 mL**
Fine dry bread crumbs	**1 cup**	**250 mL**
Grated Parmesan cheese	**2 tbsp.**	**30 mL**
Parsley flakes	**1 tsp.**	**5 mL**
Salt	**1 tsp.**	**5 mL**
Pepper	**1/4 tsp.**	**1 mL**
Paprika	**1/2 tsp.**	**2 mL**
Halibut fillets	**2 lbs.**	**900 g**
Sour cream	**1 cup**	**250 mL**
Butter (or hard margarine), melted	**1/4 cup**	**60 mL**

Mix first 7 ingredients together in small bowl.

Dip fish fillets into sour cream then into crumb mixture. Place on well-greased shallow baking pan.

Drizzle with melted butter. Bake in 500°F (260°C) oven for 10 to 12 minutes until fish flakes easily when fork tested. Serves 4 to 6.

1 serving: *490 Calories; 25 g Total Fat (7 g Mono, 2.5 g Poly, 13 g Sat); 105 mg Cholesterol; 21 g Carbohydrate; 1 g Fibre; 44 g Protein; 1350 mg Sodium*

Main Courses.
First published in September 1989.

Salmon Polenta Skewers

Polenta, ham-wrapped salmon and tender-crisp vegetables make quite an eye-catching meal. Serve with grilled vegetables or salad.

Italian dressing	1/4 cup	60 mL
Sun-dried tomato pesto	1 tbsp.	15 mL
Deli ham slices, each cut into 4 strips (about 1 inch, 2.5 cm, wide)	4	4
Fresh (or frozen, thawed) salmon fillet, skin removed, cut into 1 1/2 inch (3.8 cm) cubes	1 lb.	454 g
Zucchini slices (with peel), cut 1 inch, 2.5 cm, thick, halved crosswise	8	8
Polenta cubes (1 inch, 2.5 cm, size)	16	16
Red pepper pieces (1 inch, 2.5 cm, size)	16	16
Bamboo skewers (8 inches, 20 cm, each), soaked in water for 10 minutes	8	8

Combine dressing and pesto in small cup. Set aside.

Wrap ham strips around fish pieces.

Thread fish and next 3 ingredients alternately onto skewers. Place on large plate. Brush skewers with pesto mixture. Preheat gas barbecue to medium (see Note). Cook skewers on greased grill for 10 to 12 minutes, turning occasionally, until vegetables are tender-crisp and fish flakes easily when tested with a fork. Serves 4.

1 serving: *421 Calories; 19.5 g Total Fat (8.5 g Mono, 6.4 g Poly, 2.0 g Sat); 112 mg Cholesterol; 21 g Carbohydrate; 1 g Fibre; 41 g Protein; 1520 mg Sodium*

Note: Too cold to barbecue? Use the broiler instead! Your skewers should cook in about the same length of time—just remember to turn them occasionally. Set your oven rack so that the skewers are about 3 to 4 inches (7.5 to 10 cm) away from the top element. For most ovens, this is the top rack.

Simple Suppers.
First published in February 2007.

Salmon Ball Casserole

This casserole is one of the most appetizing ways of serving salmon. Make the balls smaller if using as a second meat.

Cans of red salmon	2 x 7 1/2 oz.	2 x 213 g
Uncooked long-grain white rice	1/2 cup	125 mL
Grated carrot	1/2 cup	125 mL
Chopped onion	1/4 cup	60 mL
Large egg	1	1
Salt	1/2 tsp.	2 mL
Pepper	1/8 tsp.	0.5 mL
Can of condensed cream of mushroom soup	10 oz.	284 mL
Water	1/2 cup	125 mL

Put salmon and juice into medium size bowl. Remove skin and round bones.

Add rice, carrot, onion, egg, salt and pepper. Mix well. Shape into balls and put in casserole, leaving room for expansion. Sixteen balls are just right for 9 x 9 inch (23 x 23 cm) dish.

Mix soup and water together. Pour over top. Bake covered in 350°F (175°C) oven for about 1 hour. Serves 5 to 6.

1 serving: *210 Calories; 9 g Total Fat (0.5 g Mono, 1 g Poly, 2 g Sat); 30 mg Cholesterol; 21 g Carbohydrate; less than 1 g Fibre; 12 g Protein; 810 mg Sodium*

Casseroles.
First published in June 1982.

Shrimp Creole

A southern dish with a bit of a bite. You can add more cayenne to the sauce to make it as hot as you like.

Hard margarine (butter browns too fast)	2 tbsp.	30 mL
Chopped onion	1 cup	250 mL
Thinly sliced celery	1/2 cup	125 mL
Chopped green pepper	1/4 cup	60 mL
All-purpose flour	2 tbsp.	30 mL
Parsley flakes	1/2 tsp.	2 mL
Salt	1/4 tsp.	1 mL
Pepper	1/8 tsp.	0.5 mL
Garlic powder	1/4 tsp.	1 mL
Cayenne pepper	1/4 tsp.	1 mL
Chicken bouillon powder	2 tsp.	10 mL
Granulated sugar	2 tsp.	10 mL
Water	1 cup	250 mL
Can of diced tomatoes	14 oz.	398 mL
Can of tomato paste	5 1/2 oz.	156 mL
Bay leaf	1	1
Cooked small or medium shrimp (peeled and deveined)	1 lb.	454 g
RICE		
Long-grain white rice	1 cup	250 mL
Boiling water	2 cups	500 mL
Salt	1/2 tsp.	2 mL

Melt margarine in large saucepan. Add onion, celery and green pepper. Sauté until lightly browned.

Mix in next 8 ingredients.

Stir in water until it boils and thickens.

(continued on next page)

Fish & Seafood.
First published in April 1996.

Stir in tomatoes, tomato paste and bay leaf. Cover. Bring to a boil. Simmer gently for 20 minutes, stirring occasionally. Discard bay leaf.

Add shrimp. Cook until hot. Makes 3 1/4 cups (800 mL) sauce.

Rice: Add rice to boiling salted water in saucepan. Cover. Simmer for about 15 minutes until rice is tender and water is absorbed. Turn out onto warmed platter. Shape into a ring. Pour shrimp mixture into centre. Serves 4.

1 serving: *420 Calories; 7 g Total Fat (3 g Mono, 2.5 g Poly, 1.5 g Sat); 220 mg Cholesterol; 59 g Carbohydrate; 4 g Fibre; 30 g Protein; 1640 mg Sodium*

Pasta Paella

Paella is a Spanish dish named after the special two-handled pan in which it was originally prepared and served. Perfect for company.

Boneless, skinless chicken breast halves (about 2), diced into 3/4 inch (2 cm) pieces	1/2 lb.	225 g
Olive oil	1 tsp.	5 mL
Large garlic cloves, minced	3	3
Medium onions, chopped	2	2
Dried crushed chilies	1/2 tsp.	2 mL
Olive oil	1 tsp.	5 mL
Medium red peppers, diced	2	2
Can of diced tomatoes, with juice	28 oz.	796 mL
Can of condensed chicken broth	10 oz.	284 mL
Hot water	2 cups	500 mL
Reserved clam juice		
Salt	1 tsp.	5 mL
Coarsely ground pepper	1/2 tsp.	2 mL
Crushed saffron threads	1/4 tsp.	1 mL
Dried oregano	1/4 tsp.	1 mL
Uncooked orzo	2 cups	500 mL
Can of whole baby clams, drained, juice reserved	5 oz.	142 g
Fresh mussels, beards removed and scrubbed clean (see Note)	1 lb.	454 g
Cooked medium shrimp (peeled and deveined)	5 oz.	140 g
Frozen peas, thawed	1 cup	250 mL

Sauté chicken in first amount of oil in large non-stick skillet or Dutch oven until lightly golden. Remove to small bowl.

(continued on next page)

Low-Fat Pasta.
First published in February 2001.

Sauté garlic, onion and chilies in second amount of oil for 3 minutes until onion is soft. Add red pepper. Sauté for 2 minutes.

Add tomato, chicken broth, hot water, reserved clam juice, salt, pepper, saffron and oregano. Bring to a boil.

Add orzo and chicken. Cover. Simmer for 15 minutes.

Add clams and mussels. Cover. Simmer for 3 minutes. Add shrimp and peas. Stir. Cover. Simmer for about 3 minutes until hot. Discard any mussels that remain closed. Serves 8.

1 serving: *340 Calories; 4 g Total Fat (1.5 g Mono, 1 g Poly, 0.5 g Sat); 80 mg Cholesterol; 46 g Carbohydrate; 4 g Fibre; 25 g Protein; 1180 mg Sodium*

Note: Before cooking, discard any mussels that are open or remain open when sharply tapped.

Shrimp Mango Curry

Rich, golden yellow sauce. Delicate curry flavour with a slight chili bite. Serve over rice.

Ripe medium mango, peeled and chopped (see Tip, page 8)	1	1
Chopped onion	1/2 cup	125 mL
Diced celery	3/4 cup	175 mL
Garlic clove, minced (or 1/4 tsp., 1 mL, powder)	1	1
Butter (or hard margarine)	1 tbsp.	15 mL
All-purpose flour	3 tbsp.	45 mL
Curry paste	1 1/2 tsp.	7 mL
Chili paste (sambal oelek)	1 tsp.	5 mL
Coconut milk	1 1/3 cups	325 mL
Dark raisins	1/2 cup	125 mL
Prepared chicken broth	2 cups	500 mL
Uncooked large shrimp, peeled and deveined, tails intact (see Tip, below)	1 1/2 lbs.	680 g
Salt	1/4 tsp.	1 mL
Brown sugar, packed	1 tbsp.	15 mL

Sauté mango, onion, celery and garlic in butter in wok or frying pan on medium-high for 5 minutes until onion is golden.

Add flour, curry paste and chili paste. Stir. Cook for 1 minute, stirring frequently.

(continued on next page)

Asian Cooking.
First published in April 2011.

TIP

To devein shrimp or prawns, strip off legs and peel off shell, leaving tail intact, if desired. Using a small, sharp knife, make a shallow cut along the centre of the back. Rinse under cold water to wash out the dark vein. To devein shrimp that you want to cook in the shell, simply slit along back right through the shell to remove the vein.

Gradually add coconut milk, raisins and broth, stirring constantly, until boiling. Reduce heat. Simmer, uncovered, for 5 minutes.

Add shrimp, salt and brown sugar. Stir. Cook for 3 minutes until shrimp turns pink and is curled. Makes about 7 cups (1.75 L).

***1 cup (250 mL):** 290 Calories; 13 g Total Fat (1 g Mono, 1 g Poly, 10 g Sat); 150 mg Cholesterol; 23 g Carbohydrate; 2 g Fibre; 22 g Protein; 480 mg Sodium*

Crown Pork Roast

This attractive, elegant crown roast will be the centrepiece of the evening. An excellent item to serve for a special occasion, but remember to order it ahead.

Crown pork roast	8 lbs.	3.6 kg
Cooking oil	1 tbsp.	15 mL
Salt	1/2 tsp.	2 mL
HAZELNUT AND APRICOT STUFFING		
Bacon slices, chopped	4	4
Finely chopped onion	3/4 cup	175 mL
Coarse fresh bread crumbs	1 1/2 cups	375 mL
Chopped dried apricots	2/3 cup	150 mL
Hazelnuts (filberts), toasted (see Tip, page 58) and chopped	2/3 cup	150 mL
Orange juice	1/4 cup	60 mL
Chopped fresh thyme leaves (or 1 1/2 tsp., 7 mL, dried)	2 tbsp.	30 mL
Large egg, fork-beaten	1	1
Tart medium cooking apple (such as Granny Smith), grated	1	1
Finely grated orange zest	1 tsp.	5 mL
APPLE ORANGE GRAVY		
All-purpose flour	1/4 cup	60 mL
Orange juice	1 cup	250 mL
Prepared chicken broth	1 cup	250 mL
Applesauce	1/2 cup	125 mL
Brandy (or 3/4 tsp., 4 mL, flavouring)	3 tbsp.	45 mL
Grainy mustard	2 tbsp.	30 mL
Salt	1/4 tsp.	1 mL
Pepper	1/4 tsp.	1 mL

Place roast, bones pointing up, on greased wire rack in roasting pan. Rub with cooking oil. Sprinkle with salt. Fill cavity with large ball of foil. Cover bone tips with small pieces of foil. Cook, uncovered, in 325°F (160°C) oven for 1 hour.

(continued on next page)

The Pork Book.
First published in September 2003.

Hazelnut and Apricot Stuffing: Cook bacon and onion in frying pan on medium for about 10 minutes, stirring occasionally, until bacon is starting to brown. Transfer to large bowl.

Add next 8 ingredients. Mix well. Makes 4 cups (1 L) stuffing. Remove roast from oven. Carefully remove foil from cavity. Spoon stuffing into cavity. Press down lightly. Cook for 1 1/2 to 2 hours, covering stuffing loosely with foil for last 30 minutes, until meat thermometer inserted into thickest part of roast (not stuffing) reads 155°F (68°C) or until desired doneness. Cover with foil. Let stand for 10 minutes. Internal temperature should rise to at least 160°F (70°C). Remove foil from bones before serving.

Apple Orange Gravy: Drain all but 1/4 cup (60 mL) drippings from roasting pan. Add flour. Cook on medium for about 1 minute, stirring constantly, until combined and browned.

Add remaining 7 ingredients. Stir. Bring to a boil. Boil for about 5 minutes, stirring until thickened. Strain through sieve. Discard any solids. Makes 2 cups (500 mL) gravy. Serve with roast and stuffing. Makes 14 one-bone portions.

***1 serving:** 616 Calories; 29.2 g Total Fat (14.4 g Mono, 3.5 g Poly, 8.7 g Sat); 187 mg Cholesterol; 23 g Carbohydrate; 2 g Fibre; 61 g Protein; 571 mg Sodium*

Special Ham Fried Rice

An Asian-style rice dish with a loose mixture of shapes, colours and textures. Other leftover cooked vegetables may be substituted for the peas.

Cooking oil	1 tbsp.	15 mL
Chopped onion	2/3 cup	150 mL
Chopped celery	2/3 cup	150 mL
Cooking oil	1 tbsp.	15 mL
Large eggs	2	2
Pepper	1/8 tsp.	0.5 mL
Cold leftover cooked long-grain white rice (about 1 cup, 250 mL, uncooked)	3 cups	750 mL
Chopped leftover cooked ham (about 6 oz., 170 g)	1 cup	250 mL
Soy sauce	2 tbsp.	30 mL
Leftover cooked (or frozen, thawed) peas	1/2 cup	125 mL
Green onions, sliced	2	2

Heat wok or large frying pan on medium-high until hot. Add first amount of cooking oil. Add first amount of onion and celery. Stir-fry for about 3 minutes until onion starts to brown. Transfer to small bowl.

Add second amount of cooking oil to wok. Add eggs and pepper. Break yolks but do not scramble. Cook, without stirring, for 1 minute. Flip. Immediately start chopping egg with edge of pancake lifter until egg is in small pieces and starting to brown.

Add rice, ham and soy sauce. Stir-fry for about 2 minutes, breaking up rice, until dry and starting to brown.

Add onion mixture, peas and green onion. Stir-fry for about 1 minute until heated through. Makes 5 cups (1.25 L). Serves 4.

***1 serving:** 427 Calories; 14.2 g Total Fat (7.2 g Mono, 3.2 g Poly, 2.9 g Sat); 135 mg Cholesterol; 53 g Carbohydrate; 2 g Fibre; 20 g Protein; 1286 mg Sodium*

Recipes For Leftovers.
First published in February 2004.

Currant Thyme Pork

The aroma of this dish will have everyone rushing to the kitchen to see what's cooking.

Chopped onion	**3/4 cup**	**175 mL**
Chopped carrot	**1 1/2 cups**	**375 mL**
Chopped parsnip	**1/2 cup**	**125 mL**
Red baby potatoes, larger ones cut in half	**2 lbs.**	**900 g**
All-purpose flour	**3 tbsp.**	**45 mL**
Boneless pork shoulder butt roast, trimmed of fat and cut into 3/4 inch (2 cm) pieces	**2 lbs.**	**900 g**
Cooking oil	**1 tbsp.**	**15 mL**
Sprigs of fresh thyme	**2**	**2**
Prepared chicken broth	**1 1/2 cups**	**375 mL**
Redcurrant jelly	**1/3 cup**	**75 mL**
Garlic cloves, crushed	**6**	**6**
Salt	**1/4 tsp.**	**1 mL**
Pepper	**1/2 tsp.**	**2 mL**
Chopped green onion	**1/4 cup**	**60 mL**

Layer first 4 ingredients, in order given, in 4 to 5 quart (4 to 5 L) slow cooker.

Measure flour into large resealable freezer bag. Add 1/2 of pork. Seal bag. Toss until coated. Repeat with remaining pork. Heat cooking oil in large frying pan on medium-high. Add pork in 2 batches. Cook for 8 to 10 minutes per batch, stirring occasionally, until browned. Scatter evenly on top of potatoes. Place thyme sprigs on top of pork.

(continued on next page)

New Make-Ahead Meals.
First published in April 2013.

Combine next 5 ingredients in small bowl. Pour over pork. Do not stir. Cover. Cook on Low for 8 to 10 hours or on High for 4 to 5 hours. Remove and discard thyme sprigs. Add green onion. Stir. Serves 8.

1 serving: *351 Calories; 9.7 g Total Fat (4.5 g Mono, 1.5 g Poly, 2.8 g Sat); 71 mg Cholesterol; 37 g Carbohydrate; 4 g Fibre; 28 g Protein; 343 mg Sodium*

Prep Time: 30 minutes

To Make Ahead: Chop vegetables (except potatoes) and prepare broth mixture early in day or night before. Chill in separate covered bowls. Assemble and cook as directed.

To Freeze: Do not freeze.

Curried Pork and Mango Sauce

The sauce has a nice bite to it. Delicious!

Pork tenderloin, cut into 1/2 inch (12 mm) thick medallions	1 lb.	454 g
Chili powder, sprinkle		
Cooking oil	1 tsp.	5 mL
MANGO SAUCE		
Chopped onion	1 cup	250 mL
Cooking oil	1 tsp.	5 mL
Curry paste	2 tsp.	10 mL
Can of sliced mangoes, diced, juice reserved	14 oz.	398 mL
Small red chili pepper, finely chopped (or 1/4 tsp., 1 mL, dried crushed chilies), optional	1	1
Diced zucchini, with peel	2 cups	500 mL
Diced red pepper	1 cup	250 mL
Lime juice	1 tbsp.	15 mL
Paprika	1 tsp.	5 mL
Skim evaporated milk	1/2 cup	125 mL
Coconut extract	1/2 tsp.	2 mL
Cornstarch	1 tbsp.	15 mL
Fresh pea pods (or frozen, thawed), about 6 oz. (170 g), sliced diagonally	2 1/2 cups	625 mL
Angel hair pasta	10 oz.	285 g
Boiling water	3 qts.	3 L
Cooking oil (optional)	1 tbsp.	15 mL
Salt	1 tbsp.	15 mL
Flaked coconut, toasted (see Tip, page 58)	2 tsp.	10 mL

Sprinkle both sides of each pork medallion with chili powder. Sauté pork in cooking oil in large non-stick frying pan until browned on both sides. Remove to plate. Keep warm.

(continued on next page)

One-Dish Meals.
First published in August 1999.

Mango Sauce: Sauté onion in first amount of cooking oil and curry paste in same frying pan for about 2 minutes until onion is soft.

Stir in next 6 ingredients. Cover. Cook for 4 minutes.

Combine evaporated milk, coconut extract and cornstarch in small cup. Mix well. Stir into zucchini mixture until boiling and thickened. Stir in 1/2 cup (125 mL) reserved mango juice, if needed, to thin sauce. Add pork. Simmer, uncovered, for about 8 minutes until cooked. Add pea pods. Cook for 3 to 4 minutes until tender-crisp.

Cook pasta in boiling water, second amount of cooking oil and salt in large uncovered pot or Dutch oven for 5 to 6 minutes, stirring occasionally, until tender but firm. Drain. Serve pork and mango sauce over pasta.

Sprinkle with coconut. Serves 4.

***1 serving:** 390 Calories; 12 g Total Fat (4 g Mono, 1.5 g Poly, 3 g Sat); 75 mg Cholesterol; 66 g Carbohydrate; 7 g Fibre; 37 g Protein; 1960 mg Sodium*

Pizza on the Grill

A very different treat. Use whatever meat you like.

Tea biscuit mix	2 cups	500 mL
Milk	1/2 cup	125 mL
Spaghetti or pizza sauce	1 cup	250 mL
Grated mozzarella cheese	2 cups	500 mL
Sliced fresh mushrooms	1 cup	250 mL
Sliced cooked meat, pepperoni, salami, wieners or lunchion meat, fresh or canned	1 cup	250 mL
Chopped green onion	1/2 cup	125 mL
Chopped red pepper	1/2 cup	125 mL
Grated mozzarella cheese	1 cup	250 mL

Combine biscuit mix with milk in bowl. Mix to form a soft ball. Press onto greased 12 inch (30 cm) pizza pan. Bake in hot barbecue with lid down over indirect heat (see Note) for about 15 minutes. Rotate pan at half-time. Crust should be only partially cooked.

Spread spaghetti sauce over crust.

Layer next 5 ingredients in order given.

Sprinkle with remaining mozzarella cheese. Return to barbecue. Cook the same way as for the crust until piping hot and cheese has melted, about 15 minutes. Cuts into 6 wedges.

1 wedge: *500 Calories; 28 g Total Fat (7 g Mono, 1 g Poly, 12 g Sat); 65 mg Cholesterol; 45 g Carbohydrate; 3 g Fibre; 22 g Protein; 1800 mg Sodium*

Note: The indirect cooking method is used for anything normally cooked in an oven, such as pie, cake, biscuits, bread, quickbread and Yorkshire pudding, as well as meat and poultry.

(continued on next page)

Barbecues.
First published in April 1991.

If using a gas barbecue with two burners, turn on only one burner. To bake a pie or cake, ensure temperature is correct first. Place an oven thermometer over unlit burner in closed barbecue. When temperature is reached, put item to be baked on grill over unlit burner. Bake with lid closed. To cook meat, set drip tray beneath meat on unlit side of grill. No water is necessary in drip pan. Cook with lid down. Check temperature with oven thermometer so heat can be regulated.

The lowest flame should give medium heat in a closed barbecue. A medium flame should give high heat.

Super Sausage Subs

These subs will freeze well. Simply thaw before heating or pop in your lunch bag in the morning and by noon, the sub is well thawed. Heat in the microwave for one minute. A great lunch!

Get It Together: non-stick frying pan, mixing spoon, measuring spoons, liquid measures, dry measures

1. Ground sausage meat	**1 lb.**	**454 g**
Medium green pepper, cut into slivers	**1**	**1**
Medium onion, sliced	**1**	**1**
Pepper	**1/8 tsp.**	**0.5 mL**
Paprika	**1/2 tsp.**	**2 mL**
Cayenne pepper, sprinkle		
Meatless pasta sauce	**1 cup**	**250 mL**
2. Submarine buns (10 inches, 25 cm, long), cut in half horizontally	**4**	**4**
Grated Cheddar (or mozzarella) cheese	**1 cup**	**250 mL**

1. Scramble-fry the sausage in the frying pan over medium heat for 10 minutes, breaking up any large lumps as it cooks. Drain. Add the green pepper, onion, pepper, paprika and cayenne pepper. Scramble-fry for 10 minutes until the vegetables are tender-crisp and the sausage is no longer pink. Stir in the pasta sauce. Remove from heat. Makes 3 cups (750 mL).

2. Pull out bits of bread from the soft centre of the top and bottom halves of the buns, making a shallow hollow. Divide the sausage mixture among the 4 bottom bun halves. Top each with 1/4 cup (60 mL) of the cheese. Lay the top bun halves over the filling to make a sandwich. Ready to eat. Makes 4 sandwiches.

***1 sub:** 630 Calories; 49 g Total Fat (19 g Mono, 4.5 g Poly, 19 g Sat); 115 mg Cholesterol; 33 g Carbohydrate; 4 g Fibre; 29 g Protein; 1510 mg Sodium*

Variation: These subs can be heated in the microwave oven on medium (50%) for 1 minute or wrapped with foil and heated in a 300°F (150°C) oven for 15 minutes.

Kids' Lunches.
First published in August 2012.

Crown Roast of Lamb

A gourmet feast. Perfect for any holiday occasion.

Crown lamb roast, containing 16 ribs	1	1
Salt, sprinkle		
Pepper, sprinkle		
STUFFING		
Chopped onion	1/4 cup	60 mL
Chopped celery	1/4 cup	60 mL
Butter (or hard margarine)	1/4 cup	60 mL
Dry bread crumbs	4 cups	1 L
Parsley flakes	2 tsp.	10 mL
Poultry seasoning	1 1/2 tsp.	7 mL
Salt	1/2 tsp.	2 mL
Pepper	1/8 tsp.	0.5 mL
Water, up to	1 cup	250 mL
MINT SAUCE		
Dried mint leaves, crumbled	1 tbsp.	15 mL
Boiling water	1/4 cup	60 mL
White vinegar	2 tbsp.	30 mL
Granulated sugar	2 tsp.	10 mL

Sprinkle all surfaces of meat with salt and pepper. Place meat in roaster on rack, rib ends up. Roast, uncovered (or cover if you prefer), in 325°F (160°C) oven for 1 hour.

Stuffing: Sauté onion and celery in butter until onion is clear and soft.

Mix crumbs, parsley, poultry seasoning, salt and pepper in bowl. Add onion, celery and any butter left in pan. Stir in water until dressing will hold together when squeezed in hand. Using 2 thicknesses of foil, shape over your fist. Place in centre of roast, pushing foil against sides of meat to keep stuffing from falling into drippings. Pack with stuffing. Cover dressing with foil lid. Cook extra stuffing in separate container. Add 1/4 cup (60 mL) butter (or hard margarine) and more water if too dry. Continue to roast lamb until

(continued on next page)

Holiday Entertaining.
First published in September 1987.

the degree of readiness you prefer is reached. If top of stuffing is dry, drizzle with melted butter or put all stuffing into bowl and mix with a bit of water.

Mint Sauce: Put all 4 ingredients into small saucepan. Bring to a boil. Simmer about 2 minutes. Makes 1/3 cup (75 mL) sauce. Serve hot with lamb. Serves 4.

1 serving (4 ribs): *780 Calories; 31 g Total Fat (8 g Mono, 3 g Poly, 15 g Sat); 135 mg Cholesterol; 83 g Carbohydrate; 5 g Fibre; 41 g Protein; 1260 mg Sodium*

Green Chili Quiche

Two kinds of cheese plus a mild green chili flavour. Good choice for lunch.

Pastry-lined 9 inch (23 cm) pie plate	1	1
Grated Monterey Jack cheese	1 1/2 cups	375 mL
Grated medium Cheddar cheese	1 cup	250 mL
Can of diced green chilies	4 oz.	113 g
Can of mushroom stems and pieces, drained	10 oz.	284 mL
Large eggs	3	3
Salt	1/4 tsp.	1 mL
Pepper	1/8 tsp.	0.5 mL
Ground cumin	1/4 tsp.	1 mL
Milk	1 cup	250 mL
Grated medium Cheddar cheese	1/2 cup	125 mL

In unbaked pastry shell scatter Monterey Jack cheese followed by first amount of Cheddar cheese, green chilies and mushrooms.

Beat eggs until frothy. Mix in salt, pepper and cumin. Add milk. Pour over mushrooms.

Sprinkle with remaining cheese. Bake on bottom shelf in 350°F (175°C) oven about 35 to 40 minutes until an inserted knife comes out clean. Leftovers may be frozen. Serves 4.

1 serving: *660 Calories; 45 g Total Fat (12 g Mono, 4.5 g Poly, 22 g Sat); 245 mg Cholesterol; 31 g Carbohydrate; 4 g Fibre; 31 g Protein; 1430 mg Sodium*

Lunches.
First published in April 1992.

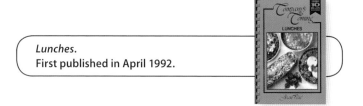

Best Roast

This "roast" would pass for a fabulous meat dish. If you are new to meatless cooking, make this recipe your first try.

Large eggs	2	2
Soy sauce	1 tbsp.	15 mL
Firm tofu, drained and patted dry, cubed	1/2 lb.	225 g
Chopped walnuts	1/2 cup	125 mL
Cooking oil	2 tbsp.	30 mL
Chopped onion	1 1/2 cups	375 mL
Chopped celery	3/4 cup	175 mL
Sliced fresh mushrooms (or 10 oz., 284 mL, can)	2 cups	500 mL
Envelope of onion soup mix	1 1/2 oz.	42 g
Dried oregano	1/2 tsp.	2 mL
Ground cumin	1/2 tsp.	2 mL
Dried basil	1/2 tsp.	2 mL
Grated Parmesan cheese	2 tbsp.	30 mL
Coarse dry bread crumbs	1 1/2 cups	375 mL

Process eggs, soy sauce and tofu in blender until smooth.

Add walnuts. Process until walnuts are ground.

Heat cooking oil in frying pan. Add onion, celery and mushrooms. Sauté until soft. Turn into bowl.

Add blender ingredients. Add remaining 6 ingredients. Mix well. Pack into greased 8 x 4 x 3 inch (20 x 10 x 7.5 cm) loaf pan. Bake in 350°F (175°C) oven for about 45 minutes. Let stand for 10 minutes. Turn out onto serving platter. Cuts into 10 slices.

1 slice: *200 Calories; 10 g Total Fat (2.5 g Mono, 3.5 g Poly, 1.5 g Sat); 45 mg Cholesterol; 21 g Carbohydrate; 2 g Fibre; 9 g Protein; 700 mg Sodium*

Meatless Cooking.
First published in April 1997.

Squash and Lentil Curry

A thick, mildly spiced lentil and vegetable curry—a fusion of fantastic flavours. Serve with flatbread and a crisp salad.

Prepared vegetable broth	**3 cups**	**750 mL**
Chopped onion	**1 1/2 cups**	**375 mL**
All-purpose flour	**2 tbsp.**	**30 mL**
Curry paste	**2 tbsp.**	**30 mL**
Garlic cloves, minced (or 1/2 tsp., 2 mL, powder)	**2**	**2**
Pepper	**1/4 tsp.**	**1 mL**
Chopped butternut squash	**2 cups**	**500 mL**
Dried green lentils, rinsed and drained	**1 1/4 cups**	**300 mL**
Chopped yam (or sweet potato)	**1 cup**	**250 mL**
Fresh spinach, stems removed, lightly packed	**3 cups**	**750 mL**
Frozen peas	**1 cup**	**250 mL**
Plain yogurt	**1/3 cup**	**75 mL**
Raw cashews, toasted (see Tip, page 58)	**1/3 cup**	**75 mL**
Salt, just a pinch		

Combine first 6 ingredients in 3 1/2 to 4 quart (3.5 to 4 L) slow cooker.

Add squash, lentils and yam. Stir well. Cover. Cook on Low for 7 to 8 hours or on High for 3 1/2 to 4 hours.

Add spinach and peas. Stir gently. Cover. Cook on High for 5 to 10 minutes until spinach is wilted and peas are heated through.

Add remaining 3 ingredients. Stir gently. Serves 6.

1 serving: *334 Calories; 6.8 g Total Fat (3.4 g Mono, 1.5 g Poly, 1.3 g Sat); 1 mg Cholesterol; 53 g Carbohydrate; 10 g Fibre; 19 g Protein; 488 mg Sodium*

Make Ahead: The night before, assemble first 9 ingredients, as directed, in slow cooker liner. Cover. Chill overnight. Cook as directed.

Slow Cooker Dinners.
First published in February 2005.

Lasagne Spirals

Cheesy spinach filling rolled in tender lasagna noodles and smothered in your favourite pasta sauce. The whole family will love these.

Lasagna noodles	**12**	**12**
Boiling water	**12 cups**	**3 L**
Salt (optional)	**1 1/2 tsp.**	**7 mL**
Large eggs	**2**	**2**
Chopped fresh spinach, stems removed, lightly packed	**2 1/4 cups**	**550 mL**
Ricotta cheese	**2 cups**	**500 mL**
Grated part-skim mozzarella cheese	**3/4 cup**	**175 mL**
Grated Parmesan cheese	**1/3 cup**	**75 mL**
Chopped fresh basil (or 1 1/2 tsp., 7 mL, dried)	**2 tbsp.**	**30 mL**
Pasta sauce	**4 cups**	**1 L**
Grated part-skim mozzarella cheese	**1 cup**	**250 mL**

Cook lasagna noodles in boiling water and salt in large uncovered pot or Dutch oven for 14 to 16 minutes, stirring occasionally, until tender but firm. Drain.

Beat eggs with fork in large bowl. Add next 5 ingredients. Stir well. Makes about 3 1/2 cups (875 mL) filling. Spread 1/3 cup (75 mL) filling on 1 lasagna noodle. Roll up, jelly roll-style, from short end. Repeat with remaining filling and noodles.

Spread 1 cup (250 mL) pasta sauce evenly in greased 9 x 13 inch (23 x 33 cm) pan. Arrange spirals, seam-side down, in single layer on top of sauce. Spoon remaining pasta sauce onto spirals. Cover with foil. Bake in 350°F (175°C) oven for about 40 minutes until heated through. Discard foil.

Sprinkle second amount of mozzarella cheese over top. Bake, uncovered, for about 15 minutes until cheese is melted. Freezes well. Makes 12 spirals.

(continued on next page)

School Days Lunches.
First published in July 2005.

***1 spiral:** 316 Calories; 14.5 g Total Fat (5.1 g Mono, 1.7 g Poly, 6.8 g Sat); 70 mg Cholesterol; 31 g Carbohydrate; 2 g Fibre; 16 g Protein; 629 mg Sodium*

Kids Can Help: Stirring spinach filling. Spreading filling on noodles and rolling them up. Spreading sauce in pan. Spooning sauce over spirals in pan. Grating cheese.

Polenta Vegetable Stacks

Plenty of polenta piled high with grilled vegetables and black beans makes for fast, fresh and healthy comfort food. Store your extra polenta, tightly wrapped, in the fridge for up to one month.

Olive oil	**1 tbsp.**	**15 mL**
Tube of plain polenta (2.2 lbs., 1 kg), cut into 8 rounds, about 1/2 inch (12 mm) thick	**1/2**	**1/2**
Slices of jalapeño Monterey Jack cheese (about 6 oz., 170 g), cut in half	**8**	**8**
Olive oil	**1 tbsp.**	**15 mL**
Thinly sliced zucchini	**1 1/2 cups**	**375 mL**
Garlic cloves, minced (or 1/2 tsp., 2 mL, powder)	**2**	**2**
Can of diced tomatoes, drained	**14 oz.**	**398 mL**
Canned black beans, rinsed and drained	**1 cup**	**250 mL**
Lime wedges, for garnish		

Preheat broiler. Heat first amount of olive oil in large frying pan on medium-high. Add polenta rounds. Cook for about 2 minutes per side until golden. Transfer to greased 9 x 13 inch (23 x 33 cm) baking dish.

Place half slice of cheese on each polenta round. Cover to keep warm.

Heat second amount of olive oil in same frying pan on medium. Add zucchini and garlic. Cook for about 3 minutes until zucchini is tender-crisp.

Add tomatoes and beans. Cook for about 1 minute until heated through. Spoon over polenta. Place remaining cheese slices on top. Broil on centre rack in oven for about 2 minutes until cheese is melted.

Garnish with lime wedges. Makes 8 stacks. Serves 4.

***1 serving:** 387 Calories; 20.3 g Total Fat (8.7 g Mono, 1.1 g Poly, 9.1 g Sat); 38 mg Cholesterol; 35.7 g Carbohydrate; 4 g Fibre; 17 g Protein; 562 mg Sodium*

Healthy In A Hurry.
First published in January 2009.

Roasted Red Pepper Pizza

A delicious, easy-to-prepare pizza with a flavourful topping.

Prebaked pizza crust (12 inch, 30 cm, diameter)	**1**	**1**
Pizza sauce	**1/3 cup**	**75 mL**
Chopped roasted red peppers	**1 cup**	**250 mL**
Fresh spinach leaves, lightly packed	**1 cup**	**250 mL**
Thinly sliced red onion	**1 cup**	**250 mL**
Chopped fresh basil (or 1 1/2 tsp., 7 mL, dried)	**2 tbsp.**	**30 mL**
Crumbled light feta cheese	**1/3 cup**	**75 mL**
Finely grated fresh Parmesan cheese	**3 tbsp.**	**45 mL**

Place pizza crust on ungreased 12 inch (30 cm) pizza pan or baking sheet. Spread pizza sauce evenly over crust.

Layer remaining 6 ingredients, in order given, over sauce. Bake on lowest rack in 475°F (240°C) oven for about 20 minutes until crust is browned. Cuts into 8 wedges.

1 wedge: *113 Calories; 2.5 g Total Fat (0 g Mono, trace Poly, 1.1 g Sat); 6 mg Cholesterol; 16 g Carbohydrate; 1 g Fibre; 5 g Protein; 506 mg Sodium*

Diabetic Dinners.
First published in October 2009.

Borscht Tart

Classic borscht flavours served in an unexpected way—this modern take on a traditional favourite packs vegetables into a tart! Surprisingly sweet with nice cayenne pepper heat.

Pastry for 9 inch (23 cm) deep dish pie shell

Cooking oil	**1 tsp.**	**5 mL**
Grated peeled beets (see Tip, page 6)	**2 cups**	**500 mL**
Chopped onion	**1 cup**	**250 mL**
Lemon juice	**1 tbsp.**	**15 mL**
Garlic cloves, minced (or 1/2 tsp., 2 mL, powder)	**2**	**2**
Cayenne pepper	**1/4 tsp.**	**1 mL**
Salt	**1/4 tsp.**	**1 mL**
Pepper	**1/4 tsp.**	**1 mL**
Large eggs, fork-beaten	**2**	**2**
Sour cream	**1 cup**	**250 mL**
Chopped walnuts, toasted (see Tip, page 58)	**1/4 cup**	**60 mL**
Chopped fresh parsley	**2 tbsp.**	**30 mL**
Sour cream, for garnish		

Roll out pastry on lightly floured surface to 1/8 inch (3 mm) thickness. Line 9 inch (23 cm) deep dish pie plate. Trim, leaving 1/2 inch (12 mm) overhang. Roll under and crimp decorative edge.

Heat cooking oil in large frying pan on medium. Add next 7 ingredients. Cook for about 10 minutes, stirring often, until onion and beets are softened. Let stand for 5 minutes to cool slightly.

(continued on next page)

Adding Vegetables to Everyday Meals.
First published in September 2012.

Combine next 3 ingredients in medium bowl. Add beet mixture. Stir. Spoon into pie shell. Bake on bottom rack in 375°F (190°C) oven for about 1 hour until knife inserted in centre comes out clean. Let stand for 5 minutes.

Sprinkle with parsley. Garnish individual servings with sour cream. Cuts into 6 wedges. Serves 6.

1 serving: *320 Calories; 23 g Total Fat (8 g Mono, 6 g Poly, 8 g Sat); 65 mg Cholesterol; 23 g Carbohydrate; 3 g Fibre; 6 g Protein; 310 mg Sodium*

Snow Pea Jicama Stir-Fry

Jicama makes an excellent substitute for water chestnuts in this colourful vegetable stir-fry. Serve with beef, chicken, pork or seafood.

Cooking oil	1 tsp.	5 mL
Thinly sliced onion	1/2 cup	125 mL
Garlic clove, minced (or 1/4 tsp., 1 mL, powder)	1	1
Italian seasoning	1 tsp.	5 mL
Bag of snow peas, trimmed	7 oz.	220 g
Thinly sliced red pepper	1 cup	250 mL
Peeled jicama, cut into 1/4 inch (6 mm) thick strips, 2 inches (5 cm) long	6 oz.	170 g
Water	1/4 cup	60 mL
Salt	1/2 tsp.	2 mL
Pepper	1/4 tsp.	1 mL
Grated lemon zest	1 tsp.	5 mL

Heat wok or large frying pan on medium-high until very hot. Add cooking oil. Add onion. Stir-fry for about 1 minute until softened. Add garlic and Italian seasoning. Stir-fry for about 30 seconds until fragrant.

Add next 3 ingredients. Stir-fry for 1 minute.

Add next 3 ingredients. Stir. Cook, covered, for about 2 minutes until snow peas are tender-crisp.

Add lemon zest. Toss. Makes about 4 cups (1 L).

1 cup (250 mL): *252 Calories; 5.6 g Total Fat (2.8 g Mono, 1.9 g Poly, 0.5 g Sat); 0 mg Cholesterol; 45 g Carbohydrate; 14 g Fibre; 9 g Protein; 1189 mg Sodium*

Choosing Sides.
First published in May 2008.

Spaghetti Squash Supreme

A fun vegetable. It may seem intimidating, but it's a cinch to prepare. May be prepared ahead and heated when needed.

Spaghetti squash	**3 lbs.**	**1.4 kg**
Broccoli florets	**2 cups**	**500 mL**
Zucchini cubes, unpeeled	**1 cup**	**250 mL**
Salted water		
Sliced carrots	**1 cup**	**250 mL**
Salted water		
Cherry tomatoes, halved	**1 cup**	**250 mL**
Butter (or hard margarine)	**2 tbsp.**	**30 mL**
Chopped green onion	**1/2 cup**	**125 mL**
Salt	**3/4 tsp.**	**4 mL**
Pepper	**1/4 tsp.**	**1 mL**
Grated Parmesan cheese, sprinkle		

Pierce skin of squash in 6 or 7 places. Set on oven rack and bake in 350°F (175°C) oven for 1 hour, until shell feels a bit soft (see Note). Remove from oven. Cool for 15 minutes. Cut in half lengthwise. Discard seeds. Using a fork, lift spaghetti strands with a scraping motion onto paper towels to drain.

Cook broccoli and zucchini in salted water for 1 minute. Cool under cold running water. Drain.

Cook carrot slices in salted water for 5 to 6 minutes. Cool under cold running water. Drain. Add to broccoli and zucchini.

Add cherry tomatoes to vegetables.

Melt butter in frying pan. Add onion, salt and pepper. Sauté until soft. Add squash strands and vegetables. Sauté until heated through.

(continued on next page)

Vegetables.
First published in April 1989.

Add cheese. Toss together. Serves 6.

1 serving: *130 Calories; 5 g Total Fat (1 g Mono, 1 g Poly, 2.5 g Sat); 10 mg Cholesterol; 22 g Carbohydrate; 4 g Fibre; 3 g Protein; 380 mg Sodium*

Note: To boil, cut squash in half lengthwise. Remove seeds. Place cut sides down in large saucepan. Pour 2 inches (5 cm) water in pan. Boil covered for about 20 minutes. Drain. Scrape with fork.

Baked Onions

The onions open like flowers while baking. Makes economical use of oven while heating main dish.

Medium onions	6	6
Butter (or hard margarine)	6 tsp.	30 mL
Brown sugar, packed	6 tsp.	30 mL
Salt, sprinkle		
Pepper, sprinkle		

Remove onion skin. Place each onion on foil square. Cut down from top to almost 1 inch (2.5 cm) from bottom. Spread apart a bit and insert 1 tsp. (5 mL) each of butter and brown sugar. Sprinkle with salt and pepper. Draw foil to top and scrunch together. Put wrapped onions in 9 x 13 inch (23 x 33 cm) pan. Bake in 350°F (175°C) oven for 1 to 1 1/2 hours until tender. Serves 6.

1 serving (1 onion): *100 Calories; 4 g Total Fat (1 g Mono, 0 g Poly, 2.5 g Sat); 10 mg Cholesterol; 16 g Carbohydrate; 2 g Fibre; 1 g Protein; 30 mg Sodium*

Prep Time: 15 minutes to assemble.

To Make Ahead: Assemble early in day or night before. Chill. To serve, bake as above. Do not freeze.

Make-Ahead Meals.
First published in September 2000.

Bacon and Cheese Spuds

Super decadent stuffing. A real filler upper!

Medium potatoes, baked (see Note)	**4**	**4**
Herb-flavoured non-fat spreadable cream cheese	**1/4 cup**	**60 mL**
Milk	**1 tbsp.**	**15 mL**
Grated light sharp Cheddar cheese	**1/4 cup**	**60 mL**
Salt	**1/4 tsp.**	**1 mL**
Pepper, sprinkle		
Bacon slices, diced	**3**	**3**
Chopped fresh mushrooms	**1/2 cup**	**125 mL**
Chopped green onion	**2 tbsp.**	**30 mL**
Grated light sharp Cheddar cheese	**1/4 cup**	**60 mL**

Cut 1/4 inch (6 mm) lengthwise from top of each potato. Scoop out pulp into medium bowl, leaving shells 1/4 inch (6 mm) thick. Discard tops once pulp is removed. Mash pulp.

Add next 5 ingredients. Beat until smooth.

Fry bacon in frying pan for 3 to 4 minutes until crisp. Remove bacon with slotted spoon. Add to potato pulp, reserving about 1 tbsp. (15 mL) for garnish.

Drain all but 1 tsp. (5 mL) fat from frying pan. Add mushrooms and green onion. Sauté until soft. Mix with potato pulp. Stuff shells.

Arrange on ungreased baking sheet. Sprinkle with second amount of Cheddar cheese. Sprinkle with reserved bacon. Bake in 350°F (175°C) oven for 20 minutes until heated through. Makes 4 stuffed potatoes.

1 stuffed potato: *260 Calories; 6 g Total Fat (1 g Mono, 0 g Poly, 3 g Sat); 20 mg Cholesterol; 39 g Carbohydrate; 4 g Fibre; 13 g Protein; 420 mg Sodium*

(continued on next page)

The Potato Book.
First published in November 2000.

Note: A medium potato is 7–8 oz. (200–225 g). To bake, wash skin of baking potato well and pierce in several places with fork. Bake, without wrapping or greasing, in 375°F (190°C) oven for 75 minutes, until soft when squeezed or fork slides in easily. Wrapping in foil produces a steamed potato with pasty texture instead of dry and fluffy, but they can be foil-wrapped when done to retain the heat until served.

Lemon Potato Packets

A variation of a popular Greek side dish, taken outside to the barbecue and cooked in individual foil packets. Use more than one colour of potato for visual interest, and serve with other Greek-inspired dishes for a themed meal.

Baby potatoes, halved	**24**	**24**
Small red onion, cut into 12 wedges (root intact)	**1**	**1**
Garlic cloves, halved	**6**	**6**
Olive (or cooking) oil	**1/3 cup**	**75 mL**
Lemon juice	**3 tbsp.**	**45 mL**
Dried oregano	**2 tsp.**	**10 mL**
Salt	**1 1/2 tsp.**	**7 mL**
Coarsely ground pepper	**1 1/2 tsp.**	**7 mL**
Grated lemon zest (see Tip, below)	**1 tsp.**	**5 mL**

Cut 6 sheets of heavy-duty (or double layer of regular) foil about 12 inches (30 cm) long. Arrange potato, onion and garlic in centre of each sheet.

Combine remaining 6 ingredients in small bowl. Drizzle over potato mixture. Fold edges of foil together over potato mixture to enclose. Fold ends to seal completely. Preheat barbecue to medium. Place packets, seam-side up, on ungreased grill. Close lid. Cook for about 25 minutes, turning occasionally, until potato and onion are tender. Makes 6 packets.

1 packet: *128 Calories; 12.5 g Total Fat (8.9 g Mono, 1.8 g Poly, 1.8 g Sat); 0 mg Cholesterol; 5 g Carbohydrate; 1 g Fibre; 1 g Protein; 583 mg Sodium*

Everyday Barbecuing.
First published in April 2010.

TIP

When a recipe calls for grated lemon zest and juice, it's easier to grate the lemon first, then juice it. Be careful not to grate down to the pith (white part of the peel), which is bitter and best avoided.

Shanghai Noodles

These noodles are quick and so easy to prepare! This spicy dish would go very well with a chicken stir-fry.

Fresh Chinese egg noodles	**12 oz.**	**340 g**
Boiling water	**12 cups**	**3 L**
Peanut (or cooking) oil	**1 tbsp.**	**15 mL**
Medium onion, cut into thin wedges	**1**	**1**
Chopped red pepper	**1 cup**	**250 mL**
Chopped green onion	**1/2 cup**	**125 mL**
Chinese satay sauce	**1/4 cup**	**60 mL**
Prepared chicken broth	**1/4 cup**	**60 mL**
Soy sauce	**2 tbsp.**	**30 mL**
Sesame oil (optional)	**2 tsp.**	**10 mL**

Cook noodles in boiling water in large uncovered pot or Dutch oven for about 2 minutes until tender but firm. Remove from heat. Stir to loosen noodles. Drain. Rinse with cold water. Drain well. Set aside.

Heat wok or large frying pan on medium-high until very hot. Add peanut oil. Add next 4 ingredients. Stir-fry for about 1 minute until fragrant.

Add noodles and remaining 3 ingredients. Stir-fry for 3 to 5 minutes until hot and onion is tender-crisp. Makes about 6 1/2 cups (1.6 L).

1 cup (250 mL): *145 Calories; 6.1 g Total Fat (2.5 g Mono, 1.7 g Poly, 1.5 g Sat); 17 mg Cholesterol; 18 g Carbohydrate; 2 g Fibre; 5 g Protein; 626 mg Sodium*

Chinese Cooking.
First published in August 2003.

Tunisian Couscous

If the idea of more rice or potatoes is boring you to tears, don't well u cooking. This exotic couscous pairs with any meat.

Water	1 3/4 cups	425 mL
Salt	1/4 tsp.	1 mL
Couscous	1 cup	250 mL
Olive (or cooking) oil	1 tbsp.	15 mL
Chopped onion	1 cup	250 mL
Finely diced carrot	1/4 cup	60 mL
Diced red pepper	1/2 cup	125 mL
Frozen peas	1/2 cup	125 mL
Brown sugar, packed	1 tsp.	5 mL
Ground cumin	1/2 tsp.	2 mL
Montreal steak spice	1/2 tsp.	2 mL
Garlic clove, minced (or 1/4 tsp., 1 mL, powder)	1	1
Ground cinnamon	1/4 tsp.	1 mL
Cayenne pepper	1/8 tsp.	0.5 mL
Lemon juice	2 tbsp.	30 mL

Combine water and salt in small saucepan. Bring to a boil. Add couscous. Stir. Remove from heat. Let stand, covered, for 5 minutes. Fluff with fork. Cover to keep warm.

Meanwhile, heat olive oil in large frying pan on medium. Add onion and carrot. Cook for about 5 minutes, stirring often, until onion is softened.

Add next 8 ingredients. Cook for about 3 minutes, stirring often, until garlic is fragrant and carrot is tender.

Add lemon juice and couscous. Stir. Makes about 4 cups (1 L).

***1/2 cup (125 mL):** 89 Calories; 2.1 g Total Fat (1.2 g Mono, 0.3 g Poly, 0.3 g Sat); 0 mg Cholesterol; 16 g Carbohydrate; 2 g Fibre; 3 g Protein; 130 mg Sodium*

30-Minute Pantry.
First published in February 2010.

Cloud Nine

This meringue is filled with a most luscious chocolate filling.

MERINGUE		
Egg whites (large), room temperature	**2**	**2**
Cream of tartar	**1/8 tsp**	**0.5 mL**
Granulated sugar	**1/2 cup**	**125 mL**
Finely chopped pecans	**1/2 cup**	**125 mL**
FILLING		
Semi-sweet chocolate chips	**1 1/3 cups**	**300 mL**
Water	**3 tbsp.**	**45 mL**
Whipping cream	**1 cup**	**250 mL**

Meringue: Beat egg whites and cream of tartar until soft peaks form. Gradually beat in sugar, beating until very stiff and glossy.

Fold in nuts. Spread on foil-lined cookie sheet in an 8-inch (20 cm) circle. Make centre about 1 inch (2.5 cm) thick with edges about 1 3/4 inches (4.5 cm) high. Bake in 275°F (140°C) oven for about 1 hour. Turn off oven. Leave meringue in oven for 1 1/2 hours. Cool and transfer to plate.

Filling: Melt chips and water in heavy saucepan over low heat, stirring. Cool.

Whip cream until stiff. Fold chocolate into cream. Pile into meringue shell. Chill 2 or 3 hours before serving. Rich enough to serve 8.

1 serving: *370 Calories; 25 g Total Fat (6 g Mono, 2 g Poly, 13 g Sat); 35 mg Cholesterol; 41 g Carbohydrate; 3 g Fibre; 5 g Protein; 25 mg Sodium*

Desserts.
First published in April 1986.

Dark Chocolate Cake

This elegant three-layer cake has a nice, fine crumb.

Boiling water	2 cups	500 mL
Cocoa, sifted if lumpy	1 cup	250 mL
All-purpose flour	2 3/4 cups	675 mL
Baking soda	2 tsp.	10 mL
Baking powder	1/2 tsp.	2 mL
Salt	1/2 tsp.	2 mL
Butter (or hard margarine), softened	1 cup	250 mL
Granulated sugar	2 1/4 cups	550 mL
Large eggs	4	4
Vanilla extract	1 1/2 tsp.	7 mL
CHOCOLATE CHEESE ICING		
Block cream cheese, softened	8 oz.	250 g
Icing (confectioner's) sugar	4 cups	1 L
Cocoa, sifted if lumpy	1/2 cup	125 mL
Butter (or hard margarine), softened	1/4 cup	60 mL
Vanilla extract	2 tsp.	10 mL

Preheat oven to 350°F (175°C). Pour boiling water over cocoa in medium bowl. Whisk until smooth. Cool.

Sift flour, baking soda, baking powder and salt onto plate.

In mixing bowl cream butter and sugar together well. Beat in eggs 1 at a time, beating until light coloured. Add vanilla.

Add flour mixture to butter mixture in 3 parts alternately with cocoa mixture in 2 parts, beginning and ending with flour. Spread into 3 greased 9 inch (23 cm) round pans. Bake in oven for 25 to 30 minutes until an inserted wooden pick comes out clean. Cool.

(continued on next page)

Cakes.
First published in September 1990.

Chocolate Cheese Icing: Put all 5 ingredients into mixing bowl. Beat slowly at first to combine, then beat at medium speed until light and fluffy. More or less icing sugar may be added as desired (see Note). More melted chocolate chips or cocoa may be added to make a darker icing. Makes about 3 1/2 cups (875 mL). Ice cake. Cuts into 10 wedges.

1 wedge: *800 Calories; 35 g Total Fat (7 g Mono, 1.5 g Poly, 21 g Sat); 170 mg Cholesterol; 119 g Carbohydrate; 5 g Fibre; 10 g Protein; 650 mg Sodium*

Note: Less icing sugar may be added. The end result will not be as sweet, and there won't be as much icing.

Cherry Butterfly Cupcakes

You'll get the very best cupcakes by using a two-layer sized cake mix, plus you'll have twelve cupcakes leftover that you can save for next time. You could also do an extra-large batch of butterfly cakes for a larger crowd—just double all the other ingredients.

Box of chocolate cake mix (2 layer size)	**1**	**1**
Cherry pie filling	**1/2 cup**	**125 mL**
Whipping cream	**1 cup**	**250 mL**
Instant vanilla pudding powder	**2 tbsp.**	**30 mL**
Fresh (or maraschino) cherries with stems	**12**	**12**

Prepare cake mix according to package directions. Fill 24 paper-lined muffin cups 3/4 full. Bake in 350°F (175°C) oven for about 20 minutes until wooden pick inserted in centre of cupcake comes out clean. Let stand in pans on wire rack until cooled completely. Trim tops of 12 cupcakes just above top of paper liner. Cut tops in half. Set aside. Scoop out and discard 1 tsp. (5 mL) from centre of each cupcake. Reserve remaining cupcakes for another use (see Note 1).

Spoon pie filling into cupcakes.

Beat whipping cream and pudding powder in medium bowl until stiff peaks form. Pipe or spoon over cupcakes. Place 2 cut halves of reserved cupcake tops into whipped cream mixture at an angle to resemble butterfly wings (see Note 2).

Arrange 1 cherry on each cupcake. Makes 12 cupcakes.

1 cupcake: *253 Calories; 14.0 g Total Fat (4.5 g Mono, 1.5 g Poly, 7.0 g Sat); 50 mg Cholesterol; 32 g Carbohydrate; 1 g Fibre; 3 g Protein; 193 mg Sodium*

Note 1: Cupcakes can be stored in an airtight container for up to 1 month in the freezer.

Note 2: Cupcakes can be frozen at this point. Thaw at room temperature and garnish with cherries.

Delicious Desserts.
First published in March 2012.

Caramel Cheesecake

An awesome dessert that will fill any craving you might have.

CRUST		
Butter (or hard margarine)	**3 tbsp.**	**45 mL**
Graham cracker crumbs	**1 cup**	**250 mL**
Brown sugar, packed	**1 tbsp.**	**15 mL**
Milk	**1 1/2 tbsp.**	**25 mL**
FILLING		
Block non-fat cream cheese (8 oz., 250 g, each)	**2**	**2**
Light ricotta cheese	**1 cup**	**250 mL**
Brown sugar, packed	**3/4 cup**	**175 mL**
All-purpose flour	**3 tbsp.**	**45 mL**
Large eggs	**2**	**2**
Vanilla extract	**1 tsp.**	**5 mL**
TOPPING		
Fat-free sour cream	**1 cup**	**250 mL**
Brown sugar, packed	**3/4 cup**	**175 mL**
Vanilla extract	**1/2 tsp.**	**2 mL**
All-purpose flour	**2 tbsp.**	**30 mL**

Crust: Melt butter in medium saucepan. Stir in graham crumbs, brown sugar and milk until well mixed. Press into bottom of 8 inch (20 cm) springform pan. Bake in 350°F (175°C) oven for 10 minutes. Cool.

Filling: Beat first 4 ingredients together in medium bowl until smooth.

Beat in eggs, 1 at a time, until just blended. Add vanilla. Mix. Pour over crust. Spread evenly. Bake for about 50 minutes until set.

Topping: Beat all 4 ingredients together in small bowl. Spread over filling. Bake for 10 minutes. Cool. Chill for several hours or overnight. Cuts into 12 pieces.

***1 piece:** 240 Calories; 6 g Total Fat (1 g Mono, 0 g Poly, 3 g Sat); 50 mg Cholesterol; 41 g Carbohydrate; less than 1 g Fibre; 7 g Protein; 260 mg Sodium*

The Cheese Book.
First published in May 2002.

Lemon Meringue Pie

This from-scratch pie is best made and eaten the same day. Lemony and light.

CRUST		
All-purpose flour	2/3 cup	150 mL
Brown sugar, packed	1 tsp.	5 mL
Salt	1/4 tsp.	1 mL
Baking powder	1/8 tsp.	0.5 mL
Lard, fairly cold	1/4 cup	60 mL
White vinegar	1/2 tsp.	2 mL
Cold water	2 tbsp.	30 mL
FILLING		
Granulated sugar	1 cup	250 mL
Cornstarch	1/3 cup	75 mL
Hot water	2 cups	500 mL
Egg yolks (large)	3	3
Juice of lemons	2	2
Butter (or hard margarine)	1 tbsp.	15 mL
Salt	1/4 tsp.	1 mL
MERINGUE		
Egg whites (large), room temperature	3	3
Cream of tartar	1/4 tsp.	1 mL
Granulated sugar	6 tbsp.	100 mL

Crust: Measure flour, brown sugar, salt and baking powder into larage bowl. Cut in lard until size of tiny peas.

Measure vinegar and water into small cup. Pour slowly over flour mixture, tossing and stirring with fork until all liquid is absorbed. Shape into ball. Roll out pastry on lightly floured surface to 1/8 inch (3 mm) thickness. Line 9 inch (23 cm) pie plate. Trim, leaving 1/2 inch (12 mm) overhang. Roll under and crimp decorative edge. Prick all over with fork. Bake in 400°F (205°C) oven about 10 to 15 minutes until lightly browned. Set aside to cool.

(continued on next page)

Pies.
First published in September 1992.

Filling: Put sugar and cornstarch in medium saucepan. Stir to mix. Stir in water and egg yolks. Stir over medium heat until it boils. Boil about 1 minute. Remove from heat.

Stir in lemon juice, butter and salt. Cool. Spoon filling into pie shell.

Meringue: Beat egg whites and cream of tartar until a stiff froth. Add sugar gradually while beating until stiff and sugar is dissolved. You should feel no graininess when rubbing a bit of meringue between fingers. Pile onto filling, being sure to seal well to pastry all around. Bake near top of 350°F (175°C) oven about 10 to 15 minutes until browned. Cuts into 8 wedges.

1 wedge: *300 Calories; 11 g Total Fat (1 g Mono, 0 g Poly, 4.5 g Sat); 85 mg Cholesterol; 49 g Carbohydrate; 0 g Fibre; 4 g Protein; 190 mg Sodium*

Strawberry Crêpes

These crêpes are lined with chocolate and fresh strawberries. Add whipped topping and a drizzle of melted chocolate for the final touch.

CRÊPES		
Large egg	**1**	**1**
Skim milk	**1/4 cup**	**60 mL**
Water	**1/3 cup**	**75 mL**
All-purpose flour	**2/3 cup**	**150 mL**
Vegetable cooking oil	**1 tbsp.**	**15 mL**
Granulated sugar	**1/4 tsp.**	**1 mL**
Salt, sprinkle		
FILLING		
Semi-sweet chocolate chips	**1/2 cup**	**125 mL**
Thinly sliced fresh strawberries	**1 cup**	**250 mL**
Granulated sugar	**1 tsp.**	**5 mL**
Frozen whipped topping, thawed	**3/4 cup**	**175 mL**
Semi-sweet chocolate chips, melted	**2 tbsp.**	**30 mL**

Crêpes: Beat egg in small bowl until frothy. Add remaining 6 ingredients. Beat until smooth. Spoon about 2 tbsp. (30 mL) into heated pan. Use teflon coated pan, or spray other type pan with no-stick cooking spray. Tip pan in circular motion to spread thinly and evenly. Brown lightly on 1 side only. Cool. Makes 8 crêpes 5 inches (12.5 cm) in diameter.

Filling: Melt first amount of chocolate chips in small saucepan over very low heat stirring often. Spread quickly over light coloured side of crêpes.

Lightly stir strawberries and sugar together in small bowl.

Place sliced strawberries, overlapping a bit, down centre of crêpes. Roll. Pipe whipped topping over crêpes. Drizzle with second amount of chocolate. Makes 8 crêpes. Single serving is 2 crêpes. Serves 4.

***1 serving:** 360 Calories; 18 g Total Fat (2.5 g Mono, 1 g Poly, 10 g Sat); 55 mg Cholesterol; 49 g Carbohydrate; 4 g Fibre; 7 g Protein; 25 mg Sodium*

Light Recipes.
First published in April 1993.

Cherry Fondue

Pleasantly sweet with a combination of cherry and almond that works well.

Can of cherry pie filling	19 oz.	540 mL
Apple juice	1/4 cup	60 mL
Milk	1/4 cup	60 mL
Almond extract	1/8 tsp.	0.5 mL
Granulated sugar	2 tbsp.	30 mL
Cornstarch	1 tbsp.	15 mL

Process all 6 ingredients in blender until smooth. Pour into medium saucepan. Heat and stir on medium-low until boiling and thickened. Carefully pour into fondue pot. Place over low heat or serve at room temperature. Makes 2 3/4 cups (675 mL).

2 tbsp. (30 mL): *35 Calories; 0 g Total Fat (0 g Mono, 0 g Poly, 0 g Sat); 0 mg Cholesterol; 9 g Carbohydrate; 0 g Fibre; 0 g Protein; 15 mg Sodium*

Suggested Dippers: peach slices, cake chunks, chocolate cookie pieces, un-iced brownie cubes…the possibilities are endless.

Fondues.
First published in November 2001.

Crispy Fruit Pizza

A dessert pizza you can eat with your fingers. Can be made the day before. This is awesome! Do not freeze.

Get It Together: a large saucepan, measuring cups, 3 mixing spoons, a hot pad, a 12 inch (30 cm) pizza pan, a small bowl, an electric mixer, measuring spoons, a small cup, a pastry brush and a medium bowl.

1. CRUST		
Butter (or hard margarine)	**1/4 cup**	**60 mL**
Large marshmallows	**32**	**32**
2. Crisp rice cereal	**5 cups**	**1.25 L**
3. TOPPING		
Block cream cheese, softened (at room temperature)	**8 oz.**	**250 g**
Icing (confectioner's) sugar	**2 cups**	**500 mL**
Cocoa, sifted if lumpy	**1/4 cup**	**60 mL**
4. Small strawberries, halved, reserve 1 whole berry	**16**	**16**
Banana, peeled and sliced	**1**	**1**
Kiwi fruit, peeled, halved lengthwise and sliced	**2**	**2**
5. GLAZE		
Apricot jam	**2 tbsp.**	**30 mL**
Water	**1 1/2 tsp.**	**7 mL**
6. Whipping cream	**1 cup**	**250 mL**
Granulated sugar	**2 tsp.**	**10 mL**
Vanilla extract	**1/2 tsp.**	**2 mL**

1. **Crust:** Combine the butter and marshmallows in the saucepan. Stir often on medium-low heat until melted.

(continued on next page)

Kids Cooking.
First published in August 1995.

2. Remove the saucepan to the hot pad. Add the cereal. Stir until it is well coated. Grease the pizza pan. Press the cereal mixture evenly over the pan with your wet fingers. Cool in the refrigerator.

3. **Topping:** Place the cream cheese, icing sugar and cocoa in the small bowl. Beat on low speed until moistened. Beat on medium speed until smooth. Spread over the cooled pizza base.

4. Arrange the strawberries, banana and kiwi fruit over the chocolate topping in a fancy design.

5. **Glaze:** Mix the jam and water in the cup. With the pastry brush, dab the fruit with the jam mixture to glaze and to prevent the fruit from turning brown.

6. Beat the whipping cream, sugar and vanilla in the medium bowl until thick. Put dabs on top of the pizza. Cuts into 8 wedges.

***1 wedge:** 550 Calories; 26 g Total Fat (4.5 g Mono, 0.5 g Poly, 16 g Sat); 80 mg Cholesterol; 79 g Carbohydrate; 3 g Fibre; 6 g Protein; 350 mg Sodium*

Monster Snake Cake

Root beer flavoured cake in the shape of a snake.

Box of white cake mix (2 layer size)	1	1
Flat root beer (see Note)	1 1/4 cups	300 mL
Large eggs	2	2
Cooking oil	1/4 cup	60 mL
FROSTING		
Envelopes of dessert topping (not prepared)	2	2
Box of instant vanilla pudding powder (4-serving size)	1	1
Milk	1 1/2 cups	375 mL
Drops of yellow liquid food colouring		
DECORATION		
Thin red licorice strip (2 inches, 5 cm, long)	1	1
Candy corn	4	4
Gumdrop candy (various colours)	90	90
Black jelly bean candies	16	16
Doughnut-shaped hard candies (such as Lifesavers), same amount as birthday candles (optional)		

Spray bottoms of 2 round 8 inch (20 cm) cake pans with no-stick cooking spray. Line with waxed paper. Spray pan and paper with no-stick cooking spray. Beat cake mix, root beer, eggs and cooking oil in large bowl for 2 to 3 minutes until smooth. Divide between pans. Bake in 350°F (175°C) oven for about 30 minutes until wooden pick inserted in centre comes out clean. Cool. Turn out onto flat surface. Remove waxed paper. Cut 3 1/4 inch (8 cm) circle in centre of each cake. Leave in place. Cut both cakes in half, making a total of 4 C-shaped pieces and 4 semi-circles (see Diagram 1). Cover cake board or heavy cardboard with foil. Arrange C-shaped pieces end to end, alternating directions to make curvy snake. Place 2 semi-circles, cut sides together, at one end of snake to make tail. Place remaining 2 semi-circles at other end of snake, slightly apart, to make open mouth (see Diagram 2).

(continued on next page)

Cook For Kids.
First published in July 2001.

Frosting: Beat dessert topping, pudding and milk in medium bowl until stiff peaks form. Beat in food colouring. Frost cut sides first with thin layer to seal in crumbs on cut edges. Frost where pieces are joined. Frost entire cake, making surface smooth and rounded.

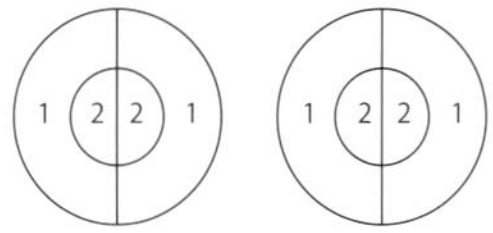

Diagram 1

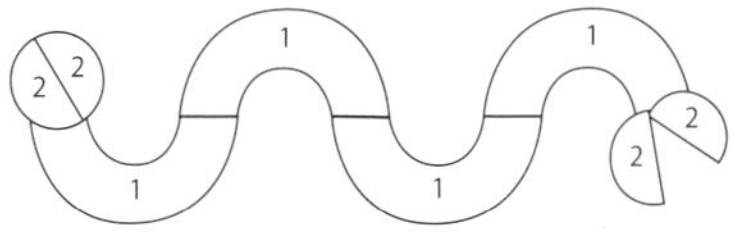

Diagram 2

Decoration: Split licorice strip halfway through for forked tongue. Place in mouth. Arrange candy corn in mouth for fangs. Arrange gumdrops and jelly beans on top and sides of cake for scales. Place birthday candles in centre of doughnut-shaped candies on top of cake. Cuts into 16 pieces.

1 piece: *290 Calories; 4.5 g Total Fat (1.5 g Mono, 1.5 g Poly; 1 g Sat); 25 mg Cholesterol; 59 g Carbohydrate; 0 g Fibre; 3 g Protein; 340 mg Sodium*

Note: To make root beer flat, stir rapidly until bubbles no longer rise to the surface.

Sweet-Spot Baby Cakes

These cutie cupcakes will be the star of the show with their lemony flavour and pretty pink frosting—plus cherries on top! You'll have more icing than you need, but having extra helps with decorating.

Get It Together: wire racks, dry and liquid measures, measuring spoons, fork, 2 medium bowls, large bowl, muffin pan, mixing spoon, zester, piping bag with medium star tip, muffin pan liners, wooden pick, electric mixer

1. All-purpose flour	**1 cup**	**250 mL**
Baking powder	**1 1/2 tsp.**	**7 mL**
Grated lemon zest	**1 tsp.**	**5 mL**
Salt	**1/8 tsp.**	**0.5 mL**
2. Butter (or hard margarine), softened	**1/3 cup**	**75 mL**
Granulated sugar	**1/2 cup**	**125 mL**
Large egg	**1**	**1**
Vanilla yogurt	**1/2 cup**	**125 mL**
CHERRY BUTTERCREAM ICING		
3. Unsweetened cherry drink powder	**1/2 tsp.**	**2 mL**
Milk	**2 tbsp.**	**30 mL**
4. Icing (confectioner's) sugar	**3 cups**	**750 mL**
Butter (or hard margarine), softened	**1/2 cup**	**125 mL**
5. Cocktail cherries with stems	**8**	**8**

1. Place oven rack in centre position. Turn oven on to 350°F (175°C). Put first 4 ingredients into medium bowl. Stir. Set aside.
2. Put butter and sugar into medium bowl. Beat until light and fluffy. Add egg. Beat well. Add half of flour mixture to butter mixture. Stir until just mixed. Add yogurt. Stir until just mixed. Add remaining flour mixture. Stir until just mixed. Fill 8 paper lined muffin cups 3/4 full. Bake in oven for about 18 minutes until wooden pick inserted in centre of a cupcake comes out clean. Put pan on stovetop. Turn oven off. Let cupcakes stand in pan for 10 minutes before removing to wire racks to cool completely.

(continued on next page)

Kids Do Baking.
First published in July 2009.

3. **Cherry Buttercream Icing:** Put drink powder and milk into large bowl. Stir until dissolved.

4. Add icing sugar and butter. Beat on low for about 30 seconds until mixed. Beat on high for about 3 minutes until light and fluffy. Spoon into piping bag fitted with medium star tip (see Tip, below). Pipe onto cupcakes.

5. Top each cupcake with 1 cocktail cherry. Makes 8 cupcakes.

***1 cupcake:** 481 Calories; 20.1 g Total Fat (5.1 g Mono, 0.8 g Poly, 12.5 g Sat); 79 mg Cholesterol; 75 g Carbohydrate; trace Fibre; 3 g Protein; 295 mg Sodium*

Cookbot 3000 Tip: If you don't have a piping bag, fill a resealable freezer bag with icing, then snip off one corner.

Star Gazers' Sundae

A delicious ice cream treat. Yum!

WARM FUDGE SAUCE		
Whipping cream	**1/3 cup**	**75 mL**
Semi-sweet chocolate baking squares (1 oz., 28 g, each), chopped	**2**	**2**
Large white marshmallows, halved	**8**	**8**
Scoops of strawberry ice cream	**8**	**8**
Frozen whipped topping, thawed	**3/4 cup**	**175 mL**
Star-shaped sprinkles	**2 tsp.**	**10 mL**
Maraschino cherries (with stems)	**4**	**4**

Warm Fudge Sauce: Combine whipping cream, chocolate and marshmallows in small saucepan. Heat and stir on medium-low for about 15 minutes until almost melted. Remove from heat. Stir until smooth. Pour into small heatproof pitcher. Makes 3/4 cup (175 mL) sauce.

Place 2 scoops of ice cream in each of 4 sundae glasses. Drizzle with sauce.

Top ice cream in each glass with whipped topping, sprinkles and 1 cherry. Serve immediately. Makes 4 sundaes.

1 sundae: *505 Calories; 26.4 g Total Fat (3.6 g Mono, 0.4 g Poly, 9.9 g Sat); 65 mg Cholesterol; 67 g Carbohydrate; trace Fibre; 6 g Protein; 104 mg Sodium*

School Days Parties.
First published in July 2004.

Spicy Dads

A spicy version of the commercial variety.

Butter (or hard margarine), softened	1 cup	250 mL
Granulated sugar	1 cup	250 mL
Brown sugar, packed	1/2 cup	125 mL
Large egg	1	1
Fancy (mild) molasses	2 tbsp.	30 mL
Vanilla extract	1 tsp.	5 mL
All-purpose flour	1 1/2 cups	375 mL
Quick-cooking rolled oats	1 1/2 cups	375 mL
Shredded coconut	1 cup	250 mL
Baking powder	1 tsp.	5 mL
Baking soda	1 tsp.	5 mL
Ground cinnamon	1 tsp.	5 mL
Ground nutmeg	1 tsp.	5 mL
Ground allspice	1 tsp.	5 mL

Cream butter and both sugars together. Beat in egg. Add molasses and vanilla.

Stir remaining ingredients together and add. Mix well. Drop by spoonfuls onto greased baking sheet. Press with floured fork. Bake in 300°F (150°C) oven until golden, about 12 minutes. Makes 6 dozen cookies.

***1 cookie:** 60 Calories; 3 g Total Fat (0.5 g Mono, 0 g Poly, 2 g Sat); 10 mg Cholesterol; 8 g Carbohydrate; 0 g Fibre; 0 g Protein; 45 mg Sodium*

Cookies.
First published in April 1988.

Peanut Butter Hide-Aways

These are definitely more impressive than regular cookies! A tasty one-bite snack that will make you popular with kids and grown-ups alike.

Butter (or hard margarine), softened	**1/2 cup**	**125 mL**
Smooth peanut butter	**1/2 cup**	**125 mL**
Granulated sugar	**1/3 cup**	**75 mL**
Brown sugar, packed	**1/3 cup**	**75 mL**
Large egg	**1**	**1**
All-purpose flour	**1 1/3 cups**	**325 mL**
Baking soda	**1/2 tsp.**	**2 mL**
Baking powder	**1 tsp.**	**5 mL**
Salt	**1/4 tsp.**	**1 mL**
Miniature peanut butter cups (or miniature chocolate candies in foil cups)	**40–45**	**40–45**

Cream butter, peanut butter and both sugars together in large bowl until light and fluffy. Beat in egg.

Combine next 4 ingredients in small bowl. Add to butter mixture. Mix until just moistened and stiff dough forms. Roll into small balls, using 1 level tbsp. (15 mL) for each. Place balls in ungreased mini-muffin pans. Bake in 375°F (190°C) oven for about 10 minutes until light golden and puffy. Remove from oven.

Peel and discard foil from peanut butter cups. Press peanut butter cups down into hot cookies. Loosen edges of cookies with tip of sharp knife. Chill in refrigerator for 20 minutes before removing from pan. If cookies are too cold and become hard to remove, tap bottom of pan several times on hard surface or let stand in pan to warm up to room temperature before removing. Makes about 3 1/2 dozen cookies.

***1 cookie:** 70 Calories; 4 g Total Fat (0.5 g Mono, 0 g Poly, 2 g Sat); 10 mg Cholesterol; 7 g Carbohydrate; 0 g Fibre; 1 g Protein; 70 mg Sodium*

The Rookie Cook.
First published in July 2002.

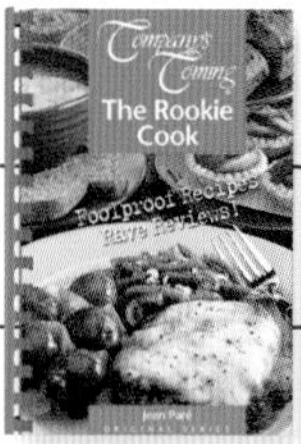

Lemon Crunch

Soda crackers provide a different yet delicious crunch to these squares.

BOTTOM LAYER		
Crushed, salted soda crackers (about 38)	**1 1/3 cups**	**325 mL**
All-purpose flour	**3/4 cup**	**175 mL**
Butter (or hard margarine), softened	**3/4 cup**	**175 mL**
Granulated sugar	**1/2 cup**	**125 mL**
Medium unsweetened coconut	**1/2 cup**	**125 mL**
Baking powder	**1 tsp.**	**5 mL**
SECOND LAYER		
Large eggs	**3**	**3**
Granulated sugar	**1 cup**	**250 mL**
Butter (or hard margarine)	**1/4 cup**	**60 mL**
Lemon juice	**1/4 cup**	**60 mL**
Grated lemon zest (see Tip, page 156)	**2 tsp.**	**10 mL**

Bottom Layer: Mix all 6 ingredients in medium bowl until crumbly. Reserve 1 cup (250 mL) for topping. Press remaining crumb mixture firmly into greased 9 x 9 inch (23 x 23 cm) pan. Bake in 350°F (175°C) oven for 15 minutes.

Second Layer: Whisk eggs in medium, heavy saucepan until frothy. Add remaining 4 ingredients. Heat and stir on medium for about 5 minutes, until thickened. Spread evenly over bottom layer. Sprinkle with reserved crumb mixture. Bake for about 20 minutes until golden brown. Let stand in pan on wire rack until cool. Cuts into 36 squares.

***1 square:** 110 Calories; 6.4 g Total Fat (1.5 g Mono, 0.2 g Poly, 4.0 g Sat); 31 mg Cholesterol; 13 g Carbohydrate; trace Fibre; 1 g Protein; 85 mg Sodium*

150 Delicious Squares.
First published in April 1981.

Brownies

Not only is this the easiest and fastest brownie to make, but it is also the best tasting ever.

Butter (or hard margarine)	1/2 cup	125 mL
Cocoa, sifted if lumpy	1/4 cup	60 mL
Large eggs	2	2
Granulated sugar	1 cup	250 mL
All-purpose flour	3/4 cup	175 mL
Chopped walnuts	1/2 cup	125 mL
Salt	1/8 tsp.	0.5 mL
ICING		
Icing (confectioner's) sugar	1 1/3 cups	325 mL
Cocoa, sifted if lumpy	1/3 cup	75 mL
Butter (or hard margarine), softened	3 tbsp.	45 mL
Hot coffee or water	5 tsp.	25 mL

In small saucepan melt butter and cocoa, stirring as it melts. Remove from heat.

In medium size bowl beat eggs until frothy. Add sugar, flour, nuts and salt. Don't stir yet. Pour cocoa mixture over top and stir all together. Scrape batter into greased 8 x 8 inch (20 x 20 cm) pan. Bake in 350°F (175°C) oven for about 30 minutes until the edges begin to show signs of pulling away from the sides of the pan.

Icing: Beat all 4 ingredients together, adding more liquid if mixture is too firm to spread easily. Spread over baked brownies. Allow to set before cutting. For a glossy look, frost while brownies are still warm. Cut into 25 squares when cool.

1 square: *140 Calories; 7 g Total Fat (2 g Mono, 1.5 g Poly, 3.5 g Sat); 30 mg Cholesterol; 18 g Carbohydrate; 0 g Fibre; 2 g Protein; 55 mg Sodium*

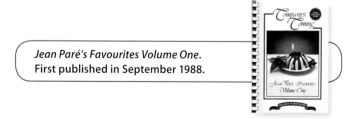

Jean Paré's Favourites Volume One.
First published in September 1988.

Fairground Squares

Just like a caramel apple—but without the stick! Look for the caramel apple wraps in the produce section of your grocery store.

Get It Together: liquid measures, sharp knife, cutting board, dry measures, 9 x 9 inch (23 x 23 cm) pan, cooking spray, medium bowl, mixing spoon, large bowl, oven mitts, wire rack

1. Diced peeled apple	**3 cups**	**750 mL**
Lemon juice	**1/4 cup**	**60 mL**
2. All-purpose flour	**1 1/2 cups**	**375 mL**
Quick-cooking rolled oats	**1 1/4 cups**	**300 mL**
Brown sugar, packed	**1/2 cup**	**125 mL**
Butter (or hard margarine)	**1 cup**	**250 mL**
3. Caramel apple wraps	**5**	**5**

1. Place oven rack in centre position. Turn oven on to 350°F (175°C). Grease pan with cooking spray. Set aside. Put apple and lemon juice into medium bowl. Stir until coated.
2. Put next 3 ingredients into large bowl. Stir. Rub in butter with your fingers until mixture resembles coarse crumbs. Press 2/3 of oat mixture into bottom of baking pan. Spread apple mixture over top.
3. Place caramel wraps over apple mixture, slightly overlapping. Sprinkle remaining oat mixture over top. Press down gently. Bake for about 30 minutes until golden. Put pan on wire rack. Turn oven off. Let cool for 5 minutes. Cuts into 16 squares.

1 square: *247 Calories; 13.1 g Total Fat (2.9 g Mono, 0.4 g Poly, 8.3 g Sat); 30 mg Cholesterol; 30 g Carbohydrate; 1 g Fibre; 3 g Protein; 117 mg Sodium*

Monsieur Auk-Auk Tip: Store these squares in an airtight container or covered with plastic wrap in the refrigerator for up to 5 days. Or, store them in the freezer for up to 1 month.

Kids Do Snacks.
First published in July 2007.

Nectarine Jam

Capture the unadulterated flavour of fresh nectarines in a lovely jewel-toned jam. Bright flavours with lovely texture.

Chopped unpeeled nectarine	**6 cups**	**1.5 L**
Bottled lemon juice	**1/4 cup**	**60 mL**
Water	**1/4 cup**	**60 mL**
Box of pectin crystals	**2 oz.**	**57 g**
Granulated sugar	**4 cups**	**1 L**

Combine first 3 ingredients in Dutch oven. Bring to a boil on medium. Boil gently, uncovered, for about 10 minutes, stirring occasionally, until nectarine is softened.

Add pectin. Bring to a boil, stirring constantly.

Add sugar. Bring to a hard boil, stirring constantly. Boil hard for 1 minute, stirring constantly. Remove from heat. Skim and discard foam. Stir for 5 minutes to suspend solids. Fill 6 hot sterile 1 cup (250 mL) jars to within 1/4 inch (6 mm) of top. Remove air bubbles and adjust headspace if necessary. Wipe rims. Place hot metal lids on jars and screw on metal bands fingertip tight. Do not over-tighten. Process in boiling water bath for 15 minutes (see Note). Remove jars. Let stand at room temperature until cool. Makes about 6 1/4 cups (1.5 L).

1 tbsp. (15 mL): *35 Calories; 0 g Total Fat (0 g Mono, 0 g Poly, 0 g Sat); 0 mg Cholesterol; 9 g Carbohydrate; 0 g Fibre; 0 g Protein; 0 mg Sodium*

Note: The United States Department of Agriculture (USDA) recommends the boiling water bath method for the final preserving step for high acid foods. Half fill canner with hot water. Place jars in rack. Lower rack to bottom. Pour in enough boiling water (not directly onto jars) to cover tops with 1 inch (2.5 cm) of water. Cover. Bring to a boil. Start timing for the number of minutes required to process the food. Correct process time at highter elevations by adding 1 additional minute per 1000 feet (305 m) above sea level. Lower the heat to maintain a gentle boil. If needed, add boiling water to keep up the level. Foods such as fruits and tomatoes with high acid content should always be processed in a boiling water bath.

Easy Home Preserving.
First published in July 2013.

Spiced Plums

An old family recipe. Especially good with baked ham or cold beef. Good served over cream cheese, cottage cheese or by itself.

Fresh prune plums	**3 1/2 lbs.**	**1.6 kg**
Granulated sugar	**6 cups**	**1.5 L**
Ground cinnamon	**1 tbsp.**	**15 mL**
Ground cloves	**1 1/2 tsp.**	**7 mL**
Salt	**1/2 tsp.**	**2 mL**
White vinegar	**1 1/2 cups**	**375 mL**

Cut plums in half. Remove stones. If you don't have a food processor, cut each half into at least 8 pieces so skin won't be in large pieces when finished. If you do have a food processor (or blender), cut each half into 3 or 4 pieces. Place in large saucepan.

Add remaining ingredients. Stir on medium-high until sugar dissolves. Bring to a boil. Boil, stirring occasionally, about 5 minutes until plums are mushy. Cool. Run through food processor in batches. Some bits of skin should show. Return to saucepan. Bring to a boil once more. Boil, stirring often, until desired thickness. Pour into hot sterilized pint jars to within 1/2 inch (12 mm) of top. Place sterilized metal lids on jars and screw metal bands on securely. For added assurance against spoilage, you may choose to process in a boiling water bath for 10 minutes. Makes about 5 pints.

1 pint: *1090 Calories; 1 g Total Fat (0 g Mono, 0 g Poly, 0 g Sat); 0 mg Cholesterol; 280 g Carbohydrate; 6 g Fibre; 2 g Protein; 240 mg Sodium*

Preserves.
First published in April 1994.

Fresh Fruit Salsa

A very good condiment for roast pork or grilled fish. Will keep in the refrigerator for up to four days.

Medium mango	1	1
Large papaya	1	1
Finely chopped red onion	1/3 cup	75 mL
Small red pepper, diced	1	1
Lime juice	1/3 cup	75 mL
Diced English cucumber, with peel	3/4 cup	175 mL
Chopped fresh cilantro	1 tbsp.	15 mL
Unsweetened applesauce	2/3 cup	150 mL
Granulated sugar	1 tsp.	5 mL
Ground cinnamon	1/4 tsp.	1 mL

Fresh mint, for garnish

Peel and dice mango and papaya, with juices, into medium bowl.

Stir in next 8 ingredients. Cover. Chill for 1 hour to blend flavours.

Garnish with mint leaves if desired. Makes 3 1/2 cups (875 mL).

***1/4 cup (60 mL):** 30 Calories; 0 g Total Fat (0 g Mono, 0 g Poly, 0 g Sat); 0 mg Cholesterol; 7 g Carbohydrate; less than 1 g Fibre; 0 g Protein; 0 mg Sodium*

Diabetic Cooking.
First published in April 2007.

Mango Dressing

Dress your salad greens, veggie sticks and fresh fruit for success with this very versatile, spicy mango dressing. Store in the fridge in an airtight container for up to one week.

Fat-free sour cream	1 cup	250 mL
Frozen mango pieces	1/2 cup	125 mL
Mango chutney	1/3 cup	75 mL
Apple cider vinegar	2 tbsp.	30 mL
Salt	1/2 tsp.	2 mL
Dried crushed chilies	1/4 tsp.	1 mL

Put all 6 ingredients into blender. Process until smooth. Makes about 1 1/3 cups (325 mL).

2 tbsp. (30 mL): *81 Calories; 2.3 g Total Fat (trace Mono, trace Poly, trace Sat); 2 mg Cholesterol; 15 g Carbohydrate; trace Fibre; 1 g Protein; 364 mg Sodium*

Low-Fat Express.
First published in March 2008.

Jerk Butter

Add a little spicy heat to your grilled fish and seafood with this flavourful butter, inspired by Jamaican cuisine.

Butter, softened	**1/2 cup**	**125 mL**
Brown sugar, packed	**1 tsp.**	**5 mL**
Dried thyme	**1 tsp.**	**5 mL**
Ground allspice	**1 tsp.**	**5 mL**
Ground chipotle chili pepper	**1 tsp.**	**5 mL**
Ground ginger	**1 tsp.**	**5 mL**
Ground cinnamon	**1/4 tsp.**	**1 mL**
Pepper	**1/4 tsp.**	**1 mL**

Beat all 8 ingredients in small bowl until combined. Transfer to sheet of waxed paper. Form into 6 inch (15 cm) long log. Wrap in waxed paper. Chill for at least 1 hour until firm. Cut into 1/4 inch (6 mm) slices. Makes 24 slices.

2 slices: *72 Calories; 7.6 g Total Fat (2.0 g Mono, 0.3 g Poly, 4.8 g Sat); 20 mg Cholesterol; 1 g Carbohydrate; trace Fibre; trace Protein; 55 mg Sodium*

Catch Of The Day.
First published in April 2009.

Corn Jicama Salsa

A nice change from tomato-based salsas. Sweet and crisp thanks to the corn and jicama, with a touch of heat from the jalapeño.

Fresh corn kernels	**2 cups**	**500 mL**
Diced peeled jicama	**1 1/2 cups**	**375 mL**
Diced red pepper	**1 cup**	**250 mL**
Finely chopped red onion	**1/4 cup**	**60 mL**
Lime juice	**3 tbsp.**	**45 mL**
Chopped fresh cilantro	**2 tbsp.**	**30 mL**
Finely chopped pickled jalapeño peppers	**2 tbsp.**	**30 mL**
Grated lime zest	**1 tsp.**	**5 mL**
Ground cumin	**1/2 tsp.**	**2 mL**
Salt	**1/4 tsp.**	**1 mL**

Combine all 10 ingredients in large bowl. Let stand for 30 minutes. Makes 4 cups (1 L).

1/2 cup (125 mL): *50 Calories; 0.5 g Total Fat (0 g Mono, 0 g Poly, 0 g Sat); 0 mg Cholesterol; 11 g Carbohydrate; 3 g Fibre; 2 g Protein; 115 mg Sodium*

MEASUREMENT TABLES

Throughout this book measurements are given in Conventional and Metric measure. To compensate for differences between the two measurements due to rounding, a full metric measure is not always used. The cup used is the standard 8 fluid ounce. Temperature is given in degrees Fahrenheit and Celsius. Baking pan measurements are in inches and centimetres as well as quarts and litres. An exact metric conversion is given below as well as the working equivalent (Metric Standard Measure).

SPOONS

Conventional Measure	Metric Exact Conversion Millilitre (mL)	Metric Standard Measure Millilitre (mL)
1/8 teaspoon (tsp.)	0.6 mL	0.5 mL
1/4 teaspoon (tsp.)	1.2 mL	1 mL
1/2 teaspoon (tsp.)	2.4 mL	2 mL
1 teaspoon (tsp.)	4.7 mL	5 mL
2 teaspoons (tsp.)	9.4 mL	10 mL
1 tablespoon (tbsp.)	14.2 mL	15 mL

CUPS

Conventional Measure	Metric Exact Conversion Millilitre (mL)	Metric Standard Measure Millilitre (mL)
1/4 cup (4 tbsp.)	56.8 mL	60 mL
1/3 cup (5 1/3 tbsp.)	75.6 mL	75 mL
1/2 cup (8 tbsp.)	113.7 mL	125 mL
2/3 cup (10 2/3 tbsp.)	151.2 mL	150 mL
3/4 cup (12 tbsp.)	170.5 mL	175 mL
1 cup (16 tbsp.)	227.3 mL	250 mL
4 1/2 cups	1022.9 mL	1000 mL

DRY MEASURES

Conventional Measure	Metric Exact Conversion Grams (mL)	Metric Standard Measure Grams (mL)
1 oz.	28.3 g	28 g
2 oz.	56.7 g	57 g
3 oz.	85.0 g	85 g
4 oz.	113.4 g	125 g
5 oz.	141.7 g	140 g
6 oz.	170.1 g	170 g
7 oz.	198.4 g	200 g
8 oz.	226.8 g	250 g
16 oz.	453.6 g	500 g
32 oz.	907.2 g	1000 g

OVEN TEMPERATURES

Fahrenheit (°F)	Celsius (°C)
175°	80°
200°	95°
225°	110°
250°	120°
275°	140°
300°	150°
325°	160°
350°	175°
375°	190°
400°	205°
425°	220°
450°	230°
475°	240°
500°	260°

PANS

Conventional Inches	Metric Inches
8 x 8 inch	20 x 20 cm
9 x 9 inch	23 x 23 cm
9 x 13 inch	23 x 33 cm
10 x 15 inch	25 x 38 cm
11 x 17 inch	28 x 43 cm
8 x 2 inch round	20 x 5 cm
9 x 2 inch round	23 x 5 cm
10 x 4 1/2 inch tube	25 x 11 cm
8 x 4 x 3 inch loaf	20 x 10 x 7.5 cm
9 x 5 x 3 inch loaf	23 x 12.5 x 7.5 cm

CASSEROLES

CANADA & BRITAIN		UNITED STATES	
Standard Size Casserole	Exact Metric Measure	Standard Size Casserole	Exact Metric Measure
1 qt. (5 cups)	1.13 L	1 qt. (4 cups)	900 mL
1 1/2 qts. (7 1/2 cups)	1.69 L	1 1/2 qts. (6 cups)	1.35 L
2 qts. (10 cups)	2.25 L	2 qts. (8 cups)	1.8 L
2 1/2 qts. (12 1/2 cups)	2.81 L	2 1/2 qts. (10 cups)	2.25 L
3 qts. (15 cups)	3.38 L	3 qts. (12 cups)	2.7 L
4 qts. (20 cups)	4.5 L	4 qts. (16 cups)	3.6 L
5 qts. (25 cups)	5.63 L	5 qts. (20 cups)	4.5 L

INDEX

M

N, O

P

Q, R

S

T

V, W, Z